MW00778190

So Ya Wanna be

THE Chief?!

Twelve Lessons in Servant-Leadership

Second Edition, with an Introduction by

James J. Flaschenreim, Charter Chief (Decd.), USAF

Bob Vásquez, CMSgt (Ret), USAF

WAJBOOK PRESS

So Ya Wanna Be *THE* Chief?! Twelve Lessons in Servant Leadership

bob vásquez

Second Edition

Copyright © 2008 and 2014 by bob vásquez

All Rights Reserved

Printed Version, ISBN 978-0-9904990-2-2

Library of Congress Control Number: 2014957524

Published in the United States by Wajbook Press

Printed by CreateSpace, a DBA of On-Demand Publishing, LLC

E-book Version, 978-0-9904990-1-5

Published in the United States by Wajbook Press

Contents

Foreword

Chief. The very word epitomizes leadership and strength.

From a Native American perspective, the Chief was responsible for the very survival and success of a tribe. Chiefs would endure any hardship, sacrifice and even death if it meant the continuation of their people. Being Odawa Indian and serving almost all of our nation's Native American tribes in the last fifteen years, I've heard the harrowing accounts of the greats from Sitting Bull to Tecumseh to Chief Joseph – sometimes directly from their descendants. Those were warriors who moved mountains and spent their lives leading, protecting and empowering their people. In a modern military organization, the same observation could be made.

I served as an Air Force officer for nearly ten years, but much of what I learned about great leadership came from the experiences I had around my dad, who was a career enlisted man in the Air Force, retiring as a Master Sergeant. Being around him, his friends and those rare figures who stirred admiration and awe, called "Chiefs", were where I gathered my most vivid lessons. In fact, when my dad knew I'd been appointed to the U.S. Air Force Academy and would be an officer, he gave me one golden piece of advice. "Remember, Son, always take care of your people and they'll take care of the mission." I smiled and said, "I know, Dad." I knew this not just from his words, but by seeing those words in action throughout my childhood.

This book speaks to what it is to be a Chief, why that role is vital, how to do it well, and addresses the issue of why you, the reader, are bold enough, and crazy enough, to want that prestigious and honored position. Will this book make becoming and being a Chief easy? No. If that's what you're looking for, put this down immediately. But what Chief Bob Vásquez has done is make the process easier. And as any good warrior knows, it's important to gather every tool, every edge, and every bit of wisdom to make us better because at the end of the day, it's not about us. It's about what we can do to strengthen our people and get the mission accomplished. This book serves that purpose.

I've known Chief Vásquez for many years now and can say he is a man who is a literal fount of enthusiasm and a tireless teacher and supporter of his people. He exhibits the best form of leadership – the kind that not only inspires but also infects others with that spark as well. With clear vision, a great sense of humor and highly disciplined, he truly walks his talk when it comes to integrity and leadership. Perhaps the best thing I could say about this man is what you already know. He is *THE* Chief.

I wish you a powerful journey through these pages. I hope you take the lessons to heart but, most importantly, I hope you apply what you learn in these pages. After all, knowledge is not power – applied knowledge is power. And as Chief Vásquez himself would say,

"HEIRPOWER, Warriors!"

D.J. Eagle Bear Vanas

Entrepreneur, Speaker, Writer and Former U.S. Air Force Captain

Author of *The Tiny Warrior: A Path to Personal Discovery & Achievement*

Acknowledgements

Chief Seattle said that we're all connected. What we do affects others. If nothing else, our actions influence others. I've been blessed with having some of the best mentors anyone could want and need. I'm grateful to each.

Thanks to *THE* Chiefs, all now retired, who made me a Chief - CMSgt John Sterle, CMSAF Bob Gaylor; CMSAF Dave Campanale, CMSAF Paul Airey (deceased), CMSAF Bud Andrews, CMSAF Sam Parish, CMSAF Jim McCoy; CMSgt Bob Smith, CMSgt Roy Boudreau, CMSgt Ron White, CMSgt Frank Guidas, CMSgt (Deceased) Mac McVicar, CMSgt George Moriarty, CMSgt Jose Tavarez and Charter CMSgt Jim Flaschenriem (deceased).

Thanks to my writing mentor and good friend, DJ Eagle Bear Vanas for his "Foreword" and his continued support of what I'm trying to do.

Thanks to Mom, Dad, and my siblings, particularly my baby sister, Elva, for providing me the love and nurturing I needed to succeed as a warrior.

Special thanks to my lovely bride of thirty–six wonderful and fulfilling years, Debbie, who has always been by me in all of the assignments, TDYs, late-night calls and who gave me the greatest gift of all, my daughters, Tesa and Elyse. Thanks to Nieves and Rain, my grandbabies, who give me different eyes by which to see this wonderful world.

Lastly and mostly, I thank my God at least twice a day for the blessings I receive every day. I'll never be worthy, but I accept them as Grace.

bob vásquez!

About the Author

Bob Vásquez is currently the course director for the freshman seminar Vital Effective Character through Observation and Reflection! (VECTOR!), offered through the US Air Force Academy's Center for Character Development. He served in the Air Force for more than 30 years before retiring on 1 November 2002. Bob invested 24 of those years in Air Force bands throughout the world.

He also served as commandant of the Noncommissioned Officer Academy at March AFB,

California; Senior Enlisted Advisor to the Commander of the 92nd Airlift Wing at Fairchild AFB, Washington; Deputy Director of the Family Support Center at Ramstein AB, Germany; and Superintendent for the 86th Support Group at Ramstein.

A proud member of the Air Force Academy's team since 16 November 2002, Bob is also an adjunct professor at the University of Colorado at Colorado Springs. He's the author of Heirpower! Eight Basic Habits of Exceptionally Powerful Lieutenants, which has received many accolades from enlisted readers as well as officers throughout the Air Force.

Although he is also a musician, motivational speaker, life coach, and mentor, Bob considers his greatest accomplishments the successful raising of his daughters, Tesa and Elyse, two sons-in-law, Nathan and Jeremy, four granddaughters, Nieves, Rain, McKinley, and Marisa, growing closer to Debbie, his lovely bride of more than 36 wonderful and fulfilling years.

Introduction

I participated in a Facebook conversation among Chiefs not too long ago that concerned me. The topic had to do with how we introduce ourselves. The great majority of the comments acknowledged that those commenting introduce themselves by the Air Force Specialty Code (AFSC) or occupation they were part of: Ammo Chief, Security Forces Chief, Services Chief, etc. Although I, most assuredly, commend anyone for having pride in what they do, or did, especially in the service to their country, my concern is that *doing* is not the same as *being*.

I was taught that as a Chief I represented, and still do, ALL enlisted members of the Air Force, not just those who are members of my current AFSC. In fact, I held a few AFSCs. The one I served in the longest was the Air Force Bandsman AFSC. I'm proud to be a Band Guy! But I'm a Chief FIRST! If I see an infraction of any type being carried out by an Airman, enlisted or officer, or by anyone of a sister service for that matter, I will do what I have to do to stop or correct it. That's what Chiefs do! If I see a military person doing something outstanding, I will acknowledge that as best I can. (I carry my own coins to present to someone, just in case.)

My point is that *being* a Chief is a much bigger and deeper responsibility than being an expert at doing something. Being a Chief is about being a leader and about leading individuals, regardless of the particular job they do. Being a Chief is not a job, it's a profession. Being a Chief is about being a Professional Warrior in the Profession of Arms, which includes all of the services and all of the AFSCs the Air Force has. It's about a commitment to a duty of the highest calling that never ends.

I hope what I've written here will empower you to be a Chief, *THE* Chief, that people of all ranks, AFSCs, and service, respect because they can count on you!

First Thought!

Wow! (Big sigh!) You finally made it to the top! The top one percent of the entire enlisted force! People will now see you as their leader, even those who don't know you or work with you. Now, after all these years of looking at others' rear ends, you are the lead dog! Now you can make all those changes you've been hoping to initiate once you didn't have to worry about your tickets and their affect on your promotion! What a great feeling! STOP!

Don't let me steal those euphoric feelings from you, but before you start dreaming, if you really want to be *THE* Chief, there are a few things you should know. At least twelve things! As you read, consider that what I'm sharing with you is based on experience and that my purpose is to help you become a great servant-leader. You've probably read or heard of that term, servant-leader. A lot of people have tried to define it. Here's my take on it.

Since this book is about how to live up to a title, Chief, let me remind you that your previous title was "sergeant." If you'll recall the PFE manual, which, by the way, you don't have to even look at again for the rest of your military life (go ahead and cheer) refers to (or used to) the origin of that term as servire, from the Latin to serve. Although you'll never be called sergeant again, it is part of your official title, Chief Master Sergeant. The sergeant, noncommissioned officer, has always been considered a servant. Not necessarily by superiors, but, more importantly, by the noncommissioned officers themselves. Being a servant, in this sense, is not so much about being subordinate. It's more about being humble. It's about service before self. Service is provided by a servant, a sergeant.

The Chief in your new title designates you as a leader. You have no choice but to lead. Okay, the truth is you always have a choice, but the choice is not whether you'll lead or not, it's what type of leader you'll be. I suggest that to be effective, you'll have to be humble. Humility will enable you to live up to that most important core value of integrity, upon which all you do will rest as long as you own that title. And the central part of that title, the master, requires that you have a clear understanding of your duty and the willingness and the passion to wear that title with excellence. A Chief Master Sergeant is a servant-leader, a humble warrior, if you will.

You've already proved yourself to be a leader, that's acknowledged by the stripes on your sleeve. Your effectiveness as a servant will be acknowledged by what's in your heart. These twelve lessons will guide you and help you grow into an effective servant-leader. If you implement them, I assure you, you'll be known not just as a chief, but as *THE* Chief!

The Charter Chiefs

By James J. Flaschenriem,

Charter Chief (Deceased), USAF

One of the most significant events in Air Force Enlisted History was the creation of the rank of E-9, the CHIEF MASTER SERGEANT. The explosion of technology during and following World War II and Korea created a need for enlisted men with leadership and technical ability far above that normally expected of a Master Sergeant as well as more formal education.

Congress created the super grades as a part of the Career Compensation Act of 1958 and decreed that 1% of the enlisted force could be in pay grade E-9 and 2% in pay grade E-8. To be eligible for promotion to those grades, the enlisted man would be required to have at least 8 years enlisted service for E-8 and 10 years for E-9.

The basic intent of Congress was to relieve the grade suppression and stagnation that had resulted from higher technical needs and faulty personnel programs. Grade suppression is one of those terms created by the military that, in this case, meant that a MSgt was supervising one or more other MSgts. Stagnation speaks for itself. There was no mandatory retirement or up or out program in effect at that time.

When the Career Compensation Act of 1958 was enacted, Air Force Personnel officials did an in-depth study and grouped all career fields into one of three categories, Highly Technical, Technical, or Non-Technical. These officials then determined that the Highly Technical fields would receive more than the 1% authorized by the original bill, the Technical fields would receive about 1% and the Non-Technical fields, less than 1%.

Upon completion of that study, manpower officials went to the manning documents and selected those Master Sergeant positions that required the higher grade and changed the slots to E-8 or E-9 as appropriate. This did not create new vacancies for promotion from TSgt to MSgt as each slot converted was dropped as an E-7 and picked up as an E-8 or E-9.

The Air Force had a unique group of about 58,000 MSgts on board as a source to select the super graders. They were men who'd grown up during the great depression when it was not unusual for young men to leave school at an early age to get jobs and help support the family. What these men lacked in formal education, they made up for in experience and knowledge gained in the school of hard knocks. Many were already in the service when WWII broke out. They served through the war, remained with the Army, transferred to the Air Force in 1947, served through the Haylift of 1948, The Berlin Airlift, Integration, Korea, and the massive retraining that took place when the old propeller driven aircraft were replaced with jets as well as the explosion of technology that was taking place. They had been tried and tempered.

It was now time to make the promotions. Air Force opted to require 10 years service for promotion to E-8 and 11 years service to E-9 rather than the 8 and 10 established in the basic law. They also required that eligibles take and pass a written supervisory test with a percentile score of 90 or more. Since no such supervisory test had been written for this purpose, the supervisory portion of the Warrant Officer Test was used. That supervisory test was no problem for MSgts with good reading skills who had attended one of the NCO Academies but presented an insurmountable obstacle for others.

That supervisory test would not have been a problem for the MSgt of today but many of the MSgts of that time could not read well enough to take and pass simple tests. At that time, an enlisted man with a high school education was considered highly educated.

Many of the officers on active duty did not have a day of college behind them. The reading skills of many MSgts was so poor, they were unable to score high enough to get into the percentile rating.

As an example of the education level, I attended a 1956 NCO Academy Class of 150 of the best MSgts in Fifteenth Air Force. Their average formal education, according to their records, was 10.8 years. That was probably a year or so higher than their actual education as the records of that time reflected what the enlisted man told the classification clerk when initially interviewed for preparation of personnel records. Formal education was not a prime factor for being a good soldier.

The first promotion boards were held at command level with field grade officers as members. Quotas and selections were made by AFSC for the first time. Board members looked at demonstrated leadership and supervisory ability, supervisors' evaluations, commander's recommendations, and best qualified. In the first cycle, Air Force promoted about 625 to Chief. The greatest number of promotions went to the Aircraft Maintenance Career Field. Those 625 came to be known as the CHARTER CHIEFS. There are less than a hundred living today that we have been able to locate.

The selection boards had a difficult role to play in the original selections as enlisted men did not have many, if any, performance reports in their file. The AIRMAN PERFORMANCE RATING SYSTEM had come into being in the mid 50's. Prior to that, the only thing in the file was an entry on the service record that the individual was or was not recommended for the Good Conduct Medal made each time the individual was reassigned.

Enlisted men got very few written commendations in those days. And, human nature being what it is, many of the old timers did everything in their power to keep from having one of those new fangled performance reports written on them.

Another factor was the numbers of eligibles with many years in grade. Thousands had been promoted to MSgt during WWII and had a date of rank in 1942, 43, 44, or 45.

There were also large numbers of former officers who had been permitted to enlist in the Army Air Corps at the end of WWII in the grade of MSgt. These were mostly high school graduates who attended one of the officer training programs and were brought into the enlisted force without one day's enlisted service and no enlisted skill.

Naturally, every MSgt on board felt he should be the first one promoted. Time-in-grade had been a primary factor in promotion for years and they felt their years in grade as a MSgt made them the one the Air Force wanted as a super grader.

There were about 58,000 MSgts on board at that time and about 625 were to be promoted. It doesn't take a rocket scientist to figure out that most were not going to be promoted. The jealously among MSgts not selected was scandalous. You still hear old timers say they were so upset at not being selected, they retired or that there was a time when time-in-grade meant something.

The selections were kept under lock and key until 1 December 1959. Announcement and promotion took place that day. There were no selection numbers as you know them today. The selectee was usually informed of his selection by his commander without great fanfare or induction ceremonies and sent back to work. The promotion of this small number resulted in there being one or two Chiefs at each base at the most. The program did not explode like an atomic burst or a flowering bush in springtime. There were not enough Chiefs at any one location to make a great deal of difference and no standard of conduct or special perks had been established for them. Most of those promoted were the movers and shakers who had gravitated to the more responsible enlisted positions so they saw little change and just a very minor pay raise. The new Chief was treated more with curiosity than anything else. Most continued in the same job and continued to be addressed as Sergeant.

Prior to the promotions, many ideas for perks and standards of conduct had been bounced off the walls. High on the list was that they be addressed as Chief. I don't know why Air Staff did not adopt this term of address. Perhaps because they didn't want to be confused with the Navy Chief. Or perhaps because we still had Warrant Officers on board who were Chief Warrant Officers. Other ideas that were run through the system were that the Chief be entitled to a salute and be addressed as Sir by junior enlisted personnel, scrambled eggs on their garrison cap visor, a yellow stripe down their trouser leg, a different uniform, and special housing entitlements. None of those ideas came to fruition and the new Chief just sewed on another stripe and got a small pay raise. The program, a jewel in the rough, was cast adrift to sink or swim on its own.

In base housing assignments, the new Chief was given priority over other enlisted men of lower rank. The top 5 on the housing list, however, regardless of rank, were frozen and could not be bumped by a senior enlisted man. One Charter Chief was reassigned to a major air command headquarters in early 1967. Housing was extremely critical. The Chief put in for base housing and was 6th on the list. When his name came up for housing, he was only entitled to a two-bedroom, one bath duplex as his family consisted of his wife and three daughters, the daughters having been born within a five year period. Can you picture this Chief with three teenage daughters and his wife, a civil service nurse at the base

24

hospital, trying to get ready to go to work and school at the same time in a two-bedroom one-bath house? Needless to say, that Chief retired when he completed one year's service in the new assignment, the minimum required at that time. What a waste. And a four-striper with a son and daughter was assigned a three-bedroom unit with a bath-and-a-half.

A Charter Chief was assigned back to a major air command headquarters for an unprecedented second tour and assigned duty in a division of the Directorate of Personnel. He served in that job for over 14 months and never once met or was introduced to the Director of Personnel who was a Brigadier General from the old school. Contrast this with the treatment of the same Chief 30-some years later when he was on invitational TDY to Aviano Air Base, Italy, to speak at a MSgt Induction Ceremony. While he was there, the Chief of Staff of the United States Air Force, a very senior four star general came to the base for a farewell visit. A special luncheon was scheduled for several enlisted men and the Charter Chief was invited. When General Ryan walked into the room, he went directly to the Charter Chief, introduced himself, thanked the Charter Chief for his contribution to the Air Force, and presented the Chief with his coin. What a difference 30 years and the new officer leadership made.

But the program did swim. The Charter Chiefs served with dignity and the established highest standards of leadership. They forged the ground rules for Chiefs to come.

As additional Chiefs were promoted, Chiefs Groups came into being. The Chiefs worked together. Still addressed as Sergeant, they petitioned to be called Chief to no avail. When the first CMSAF came on the scene, he was still addressed as Sergeant. Can you imagine addressing a man like CMSAF Paul Airey as Sergeant? If he answered the phone, you wouldn't know if he was a four-stripe Sergeant or what. But in the early 70's, the Chiefs took it upon themselves to call each other Chief. Soon, the SMSgts were calling them Chief and the MSgts, and the TSgts, etc. Air Staff saw the writing on the wall and made the official term of address of an E-9 Chief.

The Senior NCO Academy came into being in the early 70's accompanied by a new caliber of officer leadership. USAF Academy graduates were becoming field grade officers and a new wave of cooperation and respect was apparent. These USAF Academy graduates had grown up with the Chief Program and shared a deep mutual respect. It was not uncommon for the Chief to have as much or more formal education as the officer. No more enlisted men who couldn't read well enough to take a simple promotion test.

Soon, other high profile Chiefs came on the scene. Senior Enlisted Advisors, Commandants of NCO Academies, Leadership Schools, and Chiefs filling Command Chief positions. These Chiefs were assigned positions that were formerly held only by commissioned officers and they excelled. During the adolescent period of the new Chief rank, the Air Force Sergeants Association was formed and matured. Their contributions to the blossoming of the Chief Program were boundless.

And so the prestige of the rank of Chief flowered and today is one of the most respected ranks in the Air Force. The Chief does not manage by fear or intimidation as the old First Sergeant did but by knowledge, training and great leadership ability.

The Charter Chiefs extend their thanks and gratitude to all those Chiefs who followed them taking up the torch and contributing to the growth and maturing of the rank of CHIEF MASTER SERGEANT over the past 48 years.

Lesson 1

You are NOT the boss!

Why, you may ask, is this lesson the first one? Because it's the most important one of the twelve. I've known too many leaders with great potential who lost everything because they hadn't considered this lesson. Remember, I just told you how important humility is to effectiveness? Often, we think that because we've "made it to the top" we are now the boss. Not that much has changed, my friend! Did you answer to someone before you were selected for promotion to CMSgt? Do you answer to someone now? Are you married? Okay, that's a different book, but if you answered "yes" you know what I mean.

Everyone is accountable to someone else. In the military or the civilian world, we all need someone to help us stay on track. And that's a good thing. Imagine, trusting ourselves to do what's right! Some of us would fail. All of us need to be accountable to someone. So, remember, you are NOT the boss!

With almost a dozen years in grade and more than thirty years in service, when I tried to emphasize a point that required me to stand up for something that may not be status quo or the norm, I often stated publicly, "What are they going to do, fire me? Send me to (fill in the blank with a place no one wants to be assigned to)?" Every time I said that, I also said a little prayer that someone of authority wouldn't hear me and take me seriously and fire me, or, maybe worse, send me to (the place mentioned previously).

My point here is that you weren't the boss before you made Chief and ya ain't the boss now! You answer to someone just as before and just as everyone else does. The real lesson, and the way to be an effective Chief, a servant-leader, is to practice the toughest of all principles; humility. Chiefs are expected to be mature. Maturity comes from humility.

If you think that being a Chief means being a celebrity, quit now! You may enjoy the pay grade while you're in service, but you'll never make the rank. There's a big difference between an E-9 and a Chief. A Chief practices humility. *THE* Chief embodies it!

The art of being humble begins with our sense of purpose. What is your purpose? Has it changed now that you're a Chief? I hope not. I hope that your purpose before was to take care of your troops and your commander. If it wasn't, we promoted the wrong person. Sorry, but that's the truth. Aldous Huxley said, "We shall know the truth and it shall make us mad." A Chief's purpose is to take care of the troops and the commander. That purpose leads to humility, to maturity, to servant-leadership, to being *THE* Chief.

Here's what I think our collective purpose, one that we individually deploy according to the work we're involved in, should be: I inspire every member of my unit to do all we can to realize the commander's vision. You are not the boss, the commander is! That's the first lesson in being an effective Chief. Humility, we often call it service before self, is the key to effectiveness in any relationship and your relationship with your commander is critical to your success and the success of your troops. This purpose statement connects you, the troops, and the commander with a unified goal. Let me elaborate a little on that purpose statement, but let me do it the way effective leaders think, that is, backward (more on that in another lesson).

There's a verse in the Bible that says, "Where there is no vision, the people perish." Vision is critical to any successful accomplishment. Come to think of it, it affects failure as well. The development of vision is a "backward" process that I'll get into later. What is your unit's vision? Where does it come from? Now, you can read books and attend seminars where people will take all of your money (or your commander's money) to explain all types of processes to develop an organizational vision statement. If you, or your unit, can afford the time and money, go! You might learn something. Here's how I look at it in my simple mind. Who is responsible for accomplishing the mission? The question was who is "responsible?" Better yet, who is accountable? Only one person; the commander! Do unit members affect the mission? Will you affect the mission? Absolutely! But the only person accountable is the commander. As a servant-leader you have to know what your commander's vision is and do your very best to see that it becomes reality.

Surely, you've heard of, if not been part of, a unit where the commander has been relieved of duty. In the vernacular, the boss got fired! There are situations beyond anyone's control, but more often than not, a primary reason commanders get fired is that the enlisted folks set him/her up for failure. What happened is that the E-9s did it to him/her. That's the truth! You, as the senior enlisted leader, the Chief, have to accept some, sometimes most, of the blame for that commander's failure. I've seen too many instances where the Chief was the reason the commander got fired. The Chief decided he/she was the boss and went about guiding the commander down the wrong path. Unfortunately, in every situation in which I've seen that occur, the Chief followed the same path and achieved the same outcome. A universal truth is you get what you give.

On the other hand, didn't your commanders have something to do with your reaching the top rung of the ladder of success? They took care of you, now it's your turn to take care of them! Do so with humility.

Vision is critical to any success. Your unit's success starts with the commander's vision. Can you affect that vision? Of course, you can! How? It takes trust. You have to develop trust between each other. But you both have to be trustworthy. And that starts with you, not the other person. When we think about developing trust we often think that it's about what others must do. Trust begins with our own attitude toward others. It goes back to the four-letter word, humility. Okay, it's spelled with more than four letters, but we often think of it in terms of a four-letter word, something we dread.

Trust is the glue that keeps relationships together. And since you are not the boss, the only way to affect the boss's vision is to be trustworthy enough that the boss will invite you to share in developing that vision. In every unit I was assigned to, the commander's vision and mine were exactly the same. They were exactly the same as soon as I left the commander's office! We may have cussed and discussed it while in private, but as soon as we were done, our vision was the same...hers! It's what some call followership.

I've also been in the opposite situation where no matter what I did, that commander would not trust me to help her develop the unit's vision. She was a second lieutenant who thought she knew it all. I failed her and she eventually got fired and thrown out of the force. If we'd been humble enough to trust each other, we both would have succeeded. Trust is a two-way street. You both have to work on it.

Back to that purpose statement...and to humility. First, you must know what the commander's vision is, then you must do all you can to inspire every member of the unit to do everything possible to realize that vision, which is now yours as well. If you think you can do anything by yourself, think again. Everything you do and touch every day has been touched, has been affected, by someone else. Here's a prophetic statement attributed to Chief Seattle (he was a real chief):

"All things are connected. Whatever befalls the earth befalls the sons of the earth. Man did not weave the web of life. He is merely a strand on it. Whatever he does to the web he does to himself."

As a Chief, you must ensure that the entire team works together to realize your collective vision. There's an old saying that, "If we don't hang together, we'll hang together." Yeah, Ben Franklin said it a little differently. This is the updated version.

Oh, by the way, Chiefs do not promote their troops, commanders do! I know that, you say. However, comma.... I easily recall sitting at my desk as the Senior Enlisted Advisor BCC (Before Command Chiefs) the day before line numbers were to be released and getting call after call from other Chiefs asking me if I had the list of new promotees. "Yes, I have it," I'd answer. "Can you tell me if so-and-so is on it, Bob?" my fellow Chief would ask. "Nope!" was my response every single time. "No? What do you mean? We're fellow Chiefs! You can tell me!" Most of my brother and sister Chiefs were responsible professionals with strong integrity. Some, unfortunately, weren't. Through past experience I knew that some would go tell their troops that they got promoted before the commander even knew.

Warriors! Commanders promote their troops, Chiefs don't! Remember, you're not the boss, the LT is! We enlisted folks often blame our commanders for the bad stuff that happens in the unit. Commanders, remember, are responsible for all that happens in their unit, good or bad. Unfortunately, it's usually the bad stuff that they mostly have to deal with on a daily basis. Oh, not that good stuff doesn't happen. But commanders are expected to make good stuff happen. When bad stuff happens, however, they're called on the carpet immediately, of have to deal with it immediately. Promoting their troops is one of the few good things commanders get to do for their troops. Don't take that away from them. Let them be the good guys for once, especially this once. We always remember how, and my whom, we were notified of promotions, don't we? Let the boss be the one to do it. Stand next to her and the troops will remember you both!

I don't want to become redundant. I think, by now, you understand the point of this lesson. You are not the boss! You have a boss. If you want to succeed, and I don't mean get promoted again, (What, are you shooting for E-10?), then humble yourself to the fact that you are a follower. The lead follower, because all of your troops are watching how you perform. Figure out what the boss expects and figure out how to behave so that everyone you work with knows that that is the direction the unit is going. It may not be easy, but it wasn't easy making Chief either, was it?

If you're thinking, "Man, I thought this book was supposed to inspire me but all it has done is depress me." Sorry. If you learn these things I'm sharing with you, the motivation will come from practicing them. A book could never provide what you'll get from doing what's right. What's right is to lead by following. You are the Chief and your troops will do what you do, not necessarily what you say. As Ralph Waldo Emerson put it, "Who you are speaks so loudly I can't hear what you're saying." Or as

John C. Maxwell puts it, "Your walk talks and your talk talks but your walk talks louder than your talk talks." Actions always speak louder than words. You expect them to be good followers so inspire them! Practice humility. Show them you don't have to be the boss to be The Chief!

War Story

A couple of NCOs came to me and told me that a brand new Chief-select in their duty section was insisting on being called "Chief" although he hadn't sewn-on yet. Now, it's not unusual for people to call chief-selects "Chief." It's a form of respect and pride in the person's achievement. But to insist on being called "Chief," when you're not, is, in my view, despicable. As the old saying goes, "What do you call a chief-select? Senior Master Sergeant." You're not a chief until you're wearing the stripes. And that's the truth!

Anyway, this person did insist on being called "Chief." After I verified it I discussed it with him and he denied everything. I made my feelings known and assumed that that would take care of the issue. It didn't. I still got reports that the behavior had not changed. Interestingly, that person's name soon became well known throughout the wing. Incredibly, soon after getting a line number, he accosted and assaulted a young female officer in the duty section. The officer pressed charges and had a long list of witnesses who were willing to step forward in her defense. The alleged behavior was so blatant that it didn't take long to substantiate the charges. That chief-select was quickly invited to join civilian life with less than E-8 stripes.

The moral of this story is, like I said before, you're not a Chief until you sew on your stripes. And even then, you're not a Chief until you understand and embody the virtue of humility. Test my theory. Find those humble Chiefs, those servant-leaders, and observe them. You'll find that they know they're not the boss, but they don't have to be. They're servant-leaders! They are *THE* Chiefs!

The 212-Degree Challenge

There's little, if any value, in learning something but not applying it. As the adage goes, "To know, but not to do, is not to know." So what I'm going to do to empower you to apply what you read from every one of these lessons is include what I call a 212-Degree Challenge. Here's why I call it that. It's a concept I borrow from a book written by Sam Parker and Mac Anderson titled 212⬚ the extra degree. I commend you to read it. It's short, but powerful. Order it at www.walkthetalk.com.

At 211 degrees, water is hot.

At 212 degrees, it boils.

And with boiling water comes steam.

And steam can power a locomotive.

The idea here is to take action to become the servant-leader you should be. Take a minute to answer the questions and be honest with yourself. You want to move your troops toward success, don't you? Give that extra measure. They will follow you. Here's how to be as powerful as a locomotive. Hey, isn't that what Superman was? Even superman wanted to be a Chief! When you get to the "212-degree plus" level you're on your way to becoming *THE* Chief!

The 212-Degree Challenge

Is my vision the boss's vision?

- 211-degrees or less

- 212-degrees plus!

Have I done today all that I can to make the boss's vision a reality?

- 211-degrees or less

- 212-degrees plus!

Have I empowered my boss to be his/her best?

- 211-degrees or less

- 212-degrees plus!

Do my troops know that I am the Chief, and not the commander?

- 211-degrees or less

- 212-degrees plus!

Bob Vásquez, CMSgt (Ret), USAF

Lesson 2

You don't know everything!

As the Chief, you're expected to know everything. Why else would you have been promoted to Chief? The truth is - and the sooner you acknowledge this, the sooner you'll be *THE* Chief - you don't know everything. In fact, the wiser you become, the more you'll realize how little you do know. The key is to know others who know. They're usually called NCOs or Airmen.

Now, how do you know what you don't know? That's sounds like a question Yogi Berra would ask, doesn't it? Learn and practice listening. Listening is not just hearing. There's more to it. If you've been a Chief a while you know that because people (your troops) believe you know everything and because someone told you you do, and you've fallen into the pit of believing you know everything, your troops will come to you for answers. What's worse is that you'll give them answers! The problem is that you don't know the questions!

Here's what happens! The Airman comes in and starts talking. You do the traditional rapport building that you were taught at the Senior NCO Academy, of course. About 23.2 seconds after the person starts talking, you, in your infinite wisdom, already start formulating the answer to the problem. You start an internal conversation at the same time you start an external conversation. The external conversation, the one the troop hears goes something like, "Yeah, uh-huh, right, hmmm...." But you stopped listening a long time ago. The internal conversation going on inside your head is something like, "I know what you mean. I've been there. You came to the right guy because I will set you straight and you'll love me forever. Let me tell you what to do." Now, that almost seems fair. Hey, you've been there and you got through it by doing what you'll be telling the troop he or she should do as soon as they stop babbling, right?

Now, go back to your PME days to the class on counseling. Oh, no, you didn't sleep through that one, did you?! Or was that the one you already knew everything about so you tuned out the instructor? One of the most important points to know about counseling is to let the person you're counseling come up with the answers. If they choose how to respond to a problem, especially if it's the right choice, they'll feel so much better about it and they'll even give you credit for it! (That's why people believe Chiefs know everything. The good ones have convinced them they do by letting them come up with their own solutions.) On the other hand, if they make the wrong decision, they'll blame you for it. Let them make it. This is win-win thinking. There I go, asking you to think again.

Now, back to listening. Most of your troops will not use the PME process of telling you what they are going to tell you, telling you, then telling you what they told you. Normally, the first part of the conversation is either background, ice breaker, or diversion. The punch-line is at the end of the conversation. If you stopped listening as soon as you assumed (and you know what that does) you knew the question, based on that assumption, chances are you gave a perfect answer to a totally different question. What's really bad is that since you knew it was the perfect answer, you started patting yourself on the back a long time ago and called it a success.

"Wait a minute!" you say. "I always validate that the troop understood the answer I gave her and that it does answer the question. I do it by asking her if she understood and she always nods her head!" Think a little bit. The Airman is young and inexperienced, especially compared to you. She came to you because she respects your vast knowledge and expansive experience and surely there was some trepidation if not down right fear, mixed with awe, in coming to you in the first place. You ask her (with all sincerity, of course) "Do you understand?" What do you expect that youngster to answer? "Naw, man, you're not even close to answering my question. Did you stop listening? Can't you do better than that?" I think not. She's going to answer, whether it's true or not, "Yes, Chief!" As soon as she walks out the door reality will sink in and she'll wonder what planet you're from and why she came to see you to begin with. She came because someone, not you, I hope, told her the Chief knows everything!

She'll immediately talk to her friends and pass on what happened. Word of mouth is the quickest and most effective advertising method. In about three minutes, everyone in the unit will know whether you're a good listener or not. This is a crucial test of an effective Chief.

Here's a question that will bum foozle all the men reading this. Hey, I know because I am one! What's the first step in the listening process? Nope. Try again. Men! It's shut up! Yeah, I know that hit you between the eyes. It should hit you between the ears. What's interesting is that the women got it on the first try! The truth is we're scripted, trained, to provide answers. "Shut up" and "listen" are foreign words to us. No kidding! Say that to a guy and he'll say, "Huh?" But that's what ya gotta do! Shut up and listen for the question which is, again, at the end of the dialogue. Then you can use the benefit of all of your wisdom to inspire the seeker to develop her own answer. You'll have done nothing, but the word will get out that you're the best and that you have all the answers. Yeah, it's a cycle. Get over it!

In truth, you will have shut up and shut down if you listen well. We use our autobiography as our database to retrieve answers to other people's problems. That's natural. To be an effective listener, and an effective

Chief, you have to understand what the other person is trying to communicate based on his or her experiences and knowledge. Effective listening requires empathy. Empathy means understanding.

It's very different from sympathy because sympathy implies judgment. When you sympathize with someone, you're saying you agree. Empathy requires understanding as objectively as possible. Now, you and I know it's impossible to be truly objective, but if you listen for understanding, not with the intent to reply, you can be more objective and answer more unemotionally. Once emotion sets in, and judgment is emotional, the answers you provide will be tinged with your biases. Can you accept someone's opinion without having to agree or disagree with it? Sure you can! That's effective! Stephen Covey says "we can agree to disagree agreeably."

I've known, and I still know, leaders who, because they've ostensibly reached the peak of their profession, expect automatic respect from those they believe are subordinate to them. The only way to gain respect is to give it. There's a very high probability that those who work with you, some would say for you, are smarter than you are. Today's young folks have access to technology and information we only dreamed of back in the day. Use that knowledge and expertise to your advantage. Ask those you supervise to teach you. It will make them feel more important and make you a hero in their eyes. They'll feel respected because you respected them.

You don't know everything but you don't need to. If you listen empathically you can accept and understand others' needs and connect them with those who can help them if it requires going outside themselves for help. How do you know who might help? Network! That's the subject of the next lesson.

War Story

I'm sitting at my desk, minding everyone else's business, when I get a phone call. It's the middle of winter at Fairchild Air Force Base. Let me tell you, it's cold! The person on the phone is an irate spouse of one of my deployed troops. They live on base and he's been gone for a while, not sure when he'll return. At first, I can't understand what she's saying because she's, literally, shouting. I do pick up on something about her kids freezing. Once I calm her down enough so that I can understand what's she's trying to say, she, vehemently, asks me how the Group Commander has the audacity to give her a ticket for not keeping her yard cleaned up. First, her husband is gone and she's got three little ones she has to watch. Most importantly, she tells me there's no gas heat in her house. That gets my attention! "No gas? What do you mean?" I ask her. Evidently, our Civil Engineers had been doing some work on the gas lines near her house and had severed the gas line to her quarters. I asked her if she'd talked to anyone. She told me she didn't know who to contact.

Here's where being *THE* Chief is fun. I get her name, address, and phone number and tell her to give me a few minutes and I'll call her back. I immediately call my colleague at CE, CMSgt Steve Garcia, and ask him to check into what the lady has told me. A few minutes later I get a call that the CE troops are on their way to take care of the problem. Before I can call her, the lady calls me back, tears in her voice, thanking me for taking care of her and her kids. They now have heat and the troops who went out to fix the problem even took time to clean up her yard. That's servant-leadership!

The lesson here is that you don't know everything. Others know a lot more than you. We often think that because we know how important it is to keep people informed, everyone does. That's not true. Whether it's technical, work-related, or life-related, you'll only know what you know. That's Yogi at his best. If you pay attention and keep your ears and your heart open, you'll learn what you need to know and connect people who can help each other.

General Gary Voellger is one of a handful of people who have the power to call me and tell me, "Chief, we have to go to war, will you come with me?" My answer, without hesitation, would be, "Where do we meet, General?" I would go to war with that man any day! That's not the story, but it leads into one.

General Voellger was probably the most humble leader I've ever worked with. Notice I say "with" and not "for." He used to constantly admonish all of his leaders to understand how important everyone in the wing was. He taught me a very important lesson that every Chief should know and pass on to his/her folks.

There is one person who, at least twice a month, becomes the most important person in the wing. It's usually a one- or two- striper sitting at a computer. At Finance! If you've ever received a paycheck, or a bank statement, now that everything is electronic, that looks like this: "$0000.00" you know what I'm talking about. Who can help you? Go ahead, call the general or the colonel! You'll get the eyes-in-the-headlights look from them or they'll send you to the Chief or the Shirt! What will they do? Call an Airman! That young Airman has the power to change your world! Luckily, they're usually willing to help.

We all play an important role in this Air Force. "None of us is more important than the other," General Voellger would constantly preach. And none of us can succeed without the help of the other. It truly is a team effort! I believe Ken Blanchard said, "None of us is as smart as all of us."

You don't know everything, and that's okay. But make it a point to get to know a lot of people who do! And learn to connect them. People will know you as *THE* Chief!

The 212-Degree Challenge

Do I listen for understanding and not to reply?

- 211-degrees or less

- 212-degrees plus!

Do I respect others' views as valid?

- 211-degrees or less

- 212-degrees plus!

Do I encourage others to give me honest answers and/or opinions?

- 211-degrees or less

- 212-degrees plus!

Am I willing to grow?

- 211-degrees or less

- 212-degrees plus!

Lesson 3

Network!

In the past few years, a term that has gained prominence in business is "networking." It seems that term has grown in popularity as high tech has grown in taking over our lives. Networking in the high tech sense means connecting computers and informational equipment so that they can be more productive, more efficient. It makes sense, doesn't it, that if one computer has the answers in a specific area and another has the answers in another area, that if they're connected they're both more valuable because they can share their information with another enquirer.

God forbid I ever equate high tech with high touch, but that's the way networking with people works too. When you connect a person who has expertise, knowledge, or experience in a certain area with another who has expertise, knowledge, or experience in another to answer the question of a third person, there's high value because that will surely lead to synergy which means that everyone gains more. And what's really cool about the whole thing is that you get credit for it! "Yo, man, the Chief does know everything!" Well, not really, but she knows how to connect a lot of people who know a lot more than she does!

Remember that old saying, "It's not what you know, it's who you know, that counts." That's true. Now, that old saying was cynical in its origin. It meant that the way to get ahead was to brown-nose the right people. In the servant-leader context it means that when you're connected with the right people you can help a lot more by merely connecting others. Connecting. Networking.

Remember my perspective on humility and maturity? Here's what often worked for me, even, and especially, as a Chief. Be humble when you ask for help. I always got the most out of people when I went to them and acknowledged my ignorance and especially when I celebrated their expertise. That old adage about catching more flies with honey than vinegar is true.

Networking is critical to your success. Don't confuse it with cronyism, though, that will work against you. Let me put this in the context of servant-leadership. What part of a high tech, and high touch, system is the most important? Some of you will say the equipment, some of you will say the user, which is true, but what are the four most feared words in our culture? "The server is down!" Okay, if those e-mails are killing you by keeping you from the important work, you might express a sigh of relief when you hear those words. But if you rely on technology like most of us do nowadays, those words will make the tiny hairs on the back of your neck go straight up.

The most important part of a network is the server! Why? Because it's what connects everything. It's the same in the high touch world you now lead. The server, you, are critical to the process because you connect everyone! That's the fun of being a Chief! You're not the boss! You don't know everything! But you can connect everyone!

I mentioned Gen Voellger, my commander at Fairchild, before. He was a Chief in general's clothing and he knew how to use this power of networking. I recall the first commander's call he held. After the briefings, he dismissed us having talked about how important networking is to the success of a wing. An NCO came over to him and told him about a problem he was having at his on-base quarters due to a hill of rock he couldn't move but had to because it was in his yard. SMSgt (at the time, he became *THE* Chief later) Jim Guidry was standing next to the General waiting to speak with him and overheard the conversation.

As the NCO finished what he was saying, Jim, kindly chimed in that since he was a CE troop he had the tools to move that rock and would gladly do it if the NCO would give him the address. General Voellger beamed! This conversation, he told both men, is what networking is all about. We all have resources that we can share with each other. The more we do that the better we all become.

Networking is about connecting all of your resources so that there's an abundance of knowledge and experience that all of the team can tap into. All of us are much smarter than any one of us. (Oh, you've heard that one before? Good, you're paying attention!) Develop those relationships. Take Airmen and NCOs to lunch. Learn their names. Get to know their families. They're the key to your effectiveness. Network!

War Story

I'm sitting at my desk in the Family Support Center at Ramstein Air Base in Germany, about 1800, or so, when the phone rings. Yeah, I'm working half days, the second 12 hours. After introducing myself, a young lady's voice, obviously frustrated, speaks to me. "Chief," the voice says, "I need help!" I quickly sit up straighter and the adrenaline starts to rush through my veins. A damsel in distress! Someone needs my help! This is what being a Chief is all about! Bring it on! I'll help you! "I need a coke machine on my floor!" she announces. A coke machine? What's that about?

"This is the Family Support Center," I reply, "are you sure you called the right number?" "This is Chief Vásquez, isn't it?" she asks. "Someone told me you'd help. I work in the building across from yours and I've tried everything I can to get a coke machine on my floor. My customers really need it. Someone told me to call you."

Well, I guess I should be flattered that I was recommended to this young lady. I ask her a few more questions, make a couple of phone calls and, Walla, the folks who own the coke machines on base agree to put

61

one in on her floor. I call her back to give her the good news and she's ecstatic! After that, every time I saw the young lady she'd go on about how I'd helped her and even called me a hero in front of a group of her peers.

Connecting people is what being a Chief is all about. I had absolutely no resources available to help in the case above, but I found them just by connecting the folks who did. Remember the Chief Seattle quote I shared with you earlier? He said it before we even dreamed of having the world wide web. In his day it was the web of life. That's the real value of developing a network, so that we can connect each other to help one another improve our lives. Connect people! Network! That's how you become *THE* Chief!

The 212-Degree Challenge

Is my purpose to connect people?

- 211-degrees or less
- 212-degrees plus!

Do I make it a point to connect people?

- 211-degrees or less
- 212-degrees plus!

Am I constantly on the lookout for who knows what?

- 211-degrees or less
- 212-degrees plus!

Do I stay connected so that I can connect others?

- 211-degrees or less
- 212-degrees plus!

Bob Vásquez, CMSgt (Ret), USAF

Lesson 4

Mentor!

Those you lead may not do what you say, but they will always do what you do. The term "mentoring" has gotten some bad press lately. I wish I could come up with a better term, but I think it serves its purpose. Mentoring is a relationship process by which a more experienced person guides a less experienced person to reach his/her own full potential. Now, if you're a grammar geek and think the previous statement is ambiguous, I did that intentionally. Really! The ambiguous part is "to reach his/her own full potential." The grammarian would ask, "Whose potential? The mentor or the protégé?" The answer is, "Yes!" The mentoring process allows both the mentor and the protégé to learn from each other. Although we see it as the more experienced mentoring the less experienced, the smart mentor will learn as much, maybe more, than the protégé.

So, how do we mentor effectively? Let me share with you what I call my PowerPact Mentoring Cycle. There are four parts to it.

1. Connect with your protégé. Get to know him/her.

As I said in the previous lesson, in the high-tech world we live in, connecting is critical. When we're connected we can share important information and we can stay in touch. As a Mentor, you have to go beyond high-tech to high-touch and connect with your protégé. Connection is the conduit for communication and communication leads to developing solid relationships.

The very best way to start the mentoring process is to connect with your protégé on his/her turf. In other words, learn where they're coming from. That may be easier said than done, particularly if you don't know your protégé very well. So what are you going to do? Get to know your protégé! That's simple enough, isn't it? Let me help you. Here's a list of things you might want to know about your protégé. WRITE THEM DOWN! You may remember all of these things in due time, but until then, write them down and have them available when you get together (connect). You'll seem smarter than you might be, and that's always a good thing!

What is their name! Now, you may think that's a stupid thing to say. Of course, I know their name! Do people have aliases? Do they have nicknames they prefer to be called than the name on your roster? Some people even hate their given name and go by something totally different than you might think. Find out how they like to be addressed!

Here's a quick story. I was a Shirt (Additional Duty Shirt) at Keesler Air Force Base for several years. I held that position in high esteem so I did everything expected with the highest professionalism I could muster. Anyway, I made sure I didn't miss a meeting or event and got to know all of the Shirts on base. You know that when a teammate departs we always have a going-away lunch or dinner. So, as it happened, one of our fellow Shirts was PCSing so we had a little gathering. As we all shook his hand at the end of the event I went up to him and said, "It's been great working with you, Mike, and I wish you only the best in your new assignment."

He was gracious and accepted my thoughts but then he hit me between the eyes. "Bob," he said, "you know my name isn't Mike, right?" What? I'd known him for several years and I'd always called him Mike. What a time to be corrected. Man, did I feel stupid. Stupid enough that I still remember after all these years. My point? Make sure you know people's names, especially if you're going to mentor them.

Having mentored a whole bunch of folks, I can safely say that what interests most people is their family. If you develop an interest in their family and show it, they will be interested in what you have to say. Does your protégé have a spouse? Children? How many? Ages? Physical/emotional challenges?

Another thing may include their birthday. I remember one of my commanders sending birthday cards to the troops. At first I thought it was silly but I soon found out that the troops appreciated his thoughtfulness. As old as I am now, I don't care about birthdays, mine, that is, but just this past birthday our new commander, Brig Gen Susan Desjardins, sent me a birthday card. "Wow," I thought when I opened it. "That was cool!" It works! Do it!

How about a person's home town? Can that connect you? That's home, Man! Next to family, most people want to talk about home. Especially if they're from a hometown that enjoys some celebrity, like a professional football or basketball team, or a movie star, etc.

All of these things may seem trivial to you but they're your protégés life. They are what make him who he is. The more you know about those little things the better you'll be able to connect. Effective mentoring, like networking, starts with connecting.

2. Agree on what area(s) you're going to mentor your protégé. Make a plan.

As I said at the beginning of this lesson, mentoring is a two-way process by which both the mentor and the protégé can learn from each other. But learn what? Imagine being stuck in a process without end! Remember the movie, "Ground Hog Day"? The same things would happen every single day. Imagine being an Airman Basic all of your life! As great as that may sound (Trust me, there will be days when you'll wish you were an Airman Basic, without leadership responsibilities.), you'd probably get tired of it after ten or twelve years. Maybe sooner.

One of the incentives for being a good Airman is that you will one day graduate and go on to bigger and crazier things! Isn't it great when you can see the light at the end of the tunnel? That being the case, don't you think it would be of benefit to establish, and agree to, a certain time period you'll be in this mentoring process? Wouldn't it help for you and your protégé to know what it is you'll be mentoring her/him on? Would a formal agreement, a pact, provide you an instrument to maintain accountability for you and your protégé? The answer to all of these questions, of course, is yes.

After connecting with you protégé, get together and decide in what areas you'll be mentoring him or her. Are you an expert at everything? Like I said before, you don't know everything, so admit it now! Although, at the beginning of our profession, we usually find one person to mentor us, as we get older we realize that we need mentors in different areas of our lives. I've got six personal mentors as I write this. They all have expertise and experience in specific areas where I need help and I go to them when I'm in need in those particular areas of my life. I've got a life coach/mentor who kicks my butt any time I need it. I've got a writing coach who encourages me and yells at me when I need it. I've got my wife to yell at me when she needs it. Okay, you catch my drift; some of us need to be yelled at!

The point here is to agree on what you'll meet for, when (I always recommend you meet at least weekly at the beginning), for how long, what you want to achieve, etc. In other words agree on a plan. And WRITE IT DOWN! I know, I've said that before, but it bears repeating because you won't unless I yell at ya! You've heard the old adage, "fail to plan and plan to fail."

3. Guide your protégé in the right direction. Implement the plan.

Connect, agree, and then guide. You see, you know how to address your protégé. You've agreed to the terms of the process. Now do it! Man, I've known so many folks who did the first two parts yet failed to follow through with the actual mentoring. How do you gain respect? By giving respect.

How do you build trust? By being trustworthy. How do you mentor effectively? By mentoring effectively!

Mentoring can be tough. The reason is that you have to be a good listener, and, as I said before, we're not trained to listen. You wanna talk! Bite your tongue. Listen for meaning and you'll be a good mentor. You may even learn something. The key to mentoring is based on the central Air Force core value of service before self. A good mentoring relationship benefits both the mentor and the protégé. The way you will benefit is by giving. Focus on what you can do for your protégé and you'll reap great benefits. If you've already been a mentor, you know I'm telling you the truth.

I know I'm becoming redundant, but, hey, this is my book! As you meet and mentor, take notes. WRITE DOWN what was said. Oh, you don't have to develop a transcript or hire one of those professional recorders you've seen in court rooms. Write down the basic things you talked about and, especially, the important issues you addressed. I commend you to agree to an action plan of some sort. To know but not to do is not to know. It doesn't help much to talk about something your protégé would like to improve on and not develop and implement an action plan. Once you've devised an improvement process WRITE IT DOWN so that you can both refer to it when needed.

4. Follow up. Measure your progress.

Man, you are becoming an effective mentor! I know because I know you're following my advice. So far...! Here's the toughest part, I think, of the mentoring process. You have to do what we all dread and fail at in most areas of our lives. You have to follow-up! Now, even if you possess a photogenic memory, there's just too much information floating around for you to remember what you said to your protégé last time you met. So, if you WROTE IT DOWN you can follow up. See, there is some value to writing stuff down. One value is that you can measure your, or your protégés, progress.

General "Skip" Rutherford, while he was commander of Air Mobility Command, used to visit his bases and ask of Airmen of all ranks and positions, "How's it going?" General Rutherford was a big guy. Often very serious. I don't know anyone who ever saw him smile. And he wore four stars on his shoulders. When he asked how things were going, people would respond, "Great, General!" His next question would always mess up even the most secure warrior, "How do you know?" Silence.

You should have agreed, in the second part of this process, on when you'll follow up. Do it! Don't assume that your protégé had the discipline to do what she said she'd do. Not that she'd intentionally fail to live up to your agreement, but life happens, you know? If she had the discipline to do what she needs to do, she wouldn't need you! Following up allows you to measure your success or progress. Otherwise, you won't know if you're on or off track.

Have you ever gone into a job where you got little guidance but were expected to perform? Okay, I know, that's pretty much every job you've ever had. Here you are doing your very best, working your tail off. Your supervisor is really working hard as well and she's got too many folks to supervise so she doesn't make the time to follow up on your progress. You, being the over-achiever, continue to get better and better at what you're doing. Eventually, you find out that your supervisor thinks you're getting worse and worse. That's the risk of not following up regularly. As long as you keep doing what you're doing you'll keep getting what you're getting. You, the Chief, have to make sure your troops are doing what they should be doing. You have to follow up!

We often mentor informally. That's okay, I suppose. We've done it that way for as long as I can remember. The question is whether we've been effective or just expeditious. If you're interested in honing the formal process I just shared with you connect with me and I'll provide you more guidance. The informal way we mentor, and, often, the most effective way, is with our actions. Ever know a person that talks a great talk, but can't live up to it? As John C. Maxwell says, "Your talk talks and your walk talks, but your walk talks louder than your talk talks." We mentor constantly by our behavior.

Imagine advocating the importance of integrity and not living up to your commitments. What will you teach those troops who are watching you? Unlike Charles Barkley, you ARE a role model and in the role of a Chief you'll be mentoring constantly. I've always said that I could assess the quality of a leader by watching his troops. People will act as leadership does. If the troops are sharp, it's because their leadership is sharp.

Do you have children? Ever wonder what you're really like? Watch your children! You've mentored them all their lives. They learned to be the way you are. Now, some folks argue with me that they didn't spend much time with their kids. Their kids were in child care most of their lives. Well, with the exception of single parents who really may not have a choice, you chose to default your parental responsibilities to the babysitter. That's still a way to mentor. Whether you're there or not, you tell them how you feel about them.

I recall some folks referring to their leaders as stealth leaders because they were never around. Often, those leaders thought they were being empowering by not being around. The message delivered by those folks is that they didn't care enough to be around. I certainly don't advocate micromanagement, that's destructive to growth, but I do advocate cheerleading. As a senior leader, I was always amazed at how grateful my troops were when I came by to visit. I did nothing but show up! But the message was clear: The Chief cares!

Mentoring is a natural continuous process. We often do it without knowing or thinking about it. I can't tell you how many times I've been introduced as a mentor by someone whom I had no idea thought of me in such a way. When that happened I quickly retrieved those old mental files trying to remember what I'd said or done and hoped it was honorable. You'll hear this again later. You are a mentor, like it or not. Make a difference, you will. You do. What kind of a difference will you make? It's your choice! Choose wisely!

War Story

As much as I loved being on active duty, one thing I could never stand and still don't enjoy, is shaving. Now, for the first few years of my military life, I didn't have to worry about that much. I can remember when I only had to shave a couple of times a week and then I had to search for whiskers. But eventually I matured and my beard started coming in and I had to shave daily. To this day I dread it!

What's shaving got to do with mentoring? Well, it has to do with setting a good example. That may be the most important mentoring you do. People will recognize you by your rank and position. Whether you're in uniform or not, on base or off, you're still a Chief and are expected to act like one and look like one. If you're *THE* Chief, the expectations will be even higher. Being a good role model is mentoring at its best. I believe we call that excellence in all we do.

As a Senior Enlisted Advisor I was expected to epitomize the military image at all times. I recall one Saturday morning, at Fairchild, when I thought I'd "chill" a little bit so I stayed home all morning. Didn't shave. I did brush my teeth, though! About midday, my lovely bride asked me to accompany her to the BX. I didn't think much about it so we went. Well, guess who else was there? You've got it! Everyone! The general, all the O-6s, the Chiefs, every Airman I knew personally and even their families. And they all noticed that I hadn't shaved. Oh, no one said anything, but I saw it in their faces. An old professor, and I do mean he was old, Dr Huey Long, once told me that "the eyes don't lie." I could see their thoughts, and they were disappointed. It was a little bit embarrassing. What was even more embarrassing were the inspections I got Monday morning. Everyone was helping me ensure I was clean-cut in uniform. I shaved every day from then until I was thrown out of service.

The lesson is simple. Like Gen George S Patton said, "We're always on parade." As a Chief, you have to look your best at all times. Yeah, it doesn't seem fair, but you wanted those stripes, didn't you? Now that you've got them you have to grow into them. You have to practice what you preach. You're being watched, so make sure you're setting the right example. Remember I defined mentoring as a relationship process by which a more experienced person guides a less experienced person? Modeling is one way we do it.

One thing you'll note as you grow more mature in daily living is that your perspective changes as time goes by. Although I still don't enjoy it, I still shave daily. The reason is different, though. One day, as I contemplated not shaving I looked in the mirror. To my surprise, my beard had turned gray. Just yesterday it had been pitch black like my hair had been two decades before. The Bible says that "gray hair is a crown of glory; it is gained by living a godly life." Really! Read Proverbs 16:31. I can live with a crown of glory. But once your beard turns gray that's just plain old age. My goal is to stay young for as long as possible. I shave more now than I used to. I'm younger now, too!

Mentor! Do it! Do it right!

The 212-Degree Challenge

Do I know my protégés well?

- 211-degrees or less

- 212-degrees plus!

Do my protégés and I have a mutually agreed-upon mentoring plan?

- 211-degrees or less

- 212-degrees plus!

Are my protégés and I living up to our agreement?

- 211-degrees or less

- 212-degrees plus!

Do I follow up with my protégés as often as I should?

- 211-degrees or less

- 212-degrees plus!

Bob Vásquez, CMSgt (Ret), USAF

Lesson 5

Take care of yourself first!

You've probably grown up trying to live up to the core values of Integrity First, Service Before Self, and Excellence in All We Do, and that's honorable. You're probably wondering how I might reconcile this lesson with the core value of Service Before Self that is critical to our success as a force.

Here's the deal. Although serving others is key to being an effective servant-leader, answer these questions, "What good are you if you're not around? How effective are you when you're ill? Can you "hang" with the troops when you're worn out? Are you perceived as an effective leader when you're not in tune with what's happening in your environment or your specialty? When you're having a bad day, does it affect those around you?

How inspiring can you be when you're not inspired yourself?"

Surely, you've taken a flight on a commercial airline. During the safety briefing the flight attendant will get to the part about the little yellow oxygen cup hitting you in the face in case the plane loses altitude quickly. The attendant tells you to don the mask on first, then take care of your kids, then breathe normally. Breath normally. Yeah, right! If that little yellow cup hits me in the face first I'm gonna say, or at least think, something I know I shouldn't. Then, after I put that little yellow cup over my nose, I'm going to commence to breath as fast as I can, it's somehow associated with Maslow's hierarchy of needs. Survival is the first need!

Now, assuming I even remember that my wife and kids are with me on that flight, I'll certainly make sure they've got their masks on too. My gut tells me that this is an especially difficult concept for moms. Dads are from the old school, "I brought you into this life, I'll take you out!" Moms will sacrifice everything for their children. Men think, "Hey we'll just have more." Okay, not really. Okay, maybe. Anyway, the idea of taking care of yourself first is credible in this situation. It probably won't take you long to don the mask. If that's the only way to breath you'll do it with incredible speed. Remember the first time you donned your gas mask and it didn't work? It's amazing what becomes a priority pretty darn fast.

Back to the flight attendant's guidance. I think what the attendant means is not so much to breathe normally, but not to panic. That's one of the vital things you learn in CPR classes, don't panic. Panic is caused by the emotional mind. Once it takes over, you can't think logically and the flight or fight instinct takes over. Not a good thing. If you take care of yourself and don't panic, doesn't it make sense that you'll be able to assess what's going on a little bit better and make right decisions? Then you'll be able to take care of others. Service before self has to begin with serving yourself first.

As a servant-leader, you have to be physically, mentally, emotionally, and spiritually healthy in order to serve others. Take care of yourself first, then you can serve others. Let me break it down for you.

Let's first talk about physical fitness. How important is it? Of course, you know you have to take care of your body as long as you're in it. You've got no place else to go! For several years now, Americans have been on this health kick. Still, we have ungodly numbers of people dying from heart attacks and strokes. Something's not right there, don't you think? I think it might be the New Year Resolution Syndrome. Ever notice that you can hardly get into the gym between the months of January and March? After March 19th you can walk in any time because there's hardly anyone there. I know my biggest problem with maintaining my physical fitness isn't so much that I don't have a program, I just won't stick with it consistently.

Is physical fitness important to taking care of yourself? Of course it is! What does it consist of? Most of us quickly develop the vision of looking like Arnold Schwarzenegger or Cindy Crawford. Arnold for the men and Cindy for the women, of course! That's okay if you have the time and can make the commitment to it. But you know what it takes to look like that? A lot of work! Most of us aren't willing to make that investment, but we still want those results. Ain't gonna happen! But you can maintain your health and even retain your girlish figure if you work at it consistently.

For years, physical fitness experts have told us that all it takes to maintain your heart in good working condition is to invest 20 minutes a day, three times a week, in aerobic exercise. Twenty minutes, three times a week. If my cypherin' is correct, that's one hour, per week. Do you know how many hours are in a week? 168. Trust me, I did the math. Is it worth investing 1/168th of your time to increase your life span? If it only increased it by one day, would it not be worth it? Well, yeah, but....

Now get off your butt. I'm not talking about lifting hundreds of pounds at the gym. Although if that's what cranks your motor, great, do it! All I'm talking about, at minimum, is taking a brisk walk for twenty minutes. Imagine! You're behind that computer you love, replying to every single e-mail you get, for hours on end. Wouldn't it be nice to get up and take a walk for twenty minutes? And if you did that twice a day wouldn't you feel better and possibly increase your life span? Simple stuff! All you need is a place to do it (outdoors is great) and a pair of walking shoes. Part of our problem, I think, is that we want to look cool while we're exercising and it becomes the priority. (I have a whole chapter on that, you'll have to wait for the next book.) You don't have to look cool to be healthy, that will come later when you are healthy!

The other part of physical fitness has to do with diet. I'll tell you now, this is the most difficult area of my life. I'd rather work out an hour a day, every day, than to give up the foods I like. I suppose what's good is to strike a balance, whatever that is. Again, you know how important it is not to eat too much fat and to eat whole grains and to drink plenty of water. I'm not an expert by any means. Get a good book that will help you eat sensibly, and not too much. I can't tell you how many times, as an Air Force Bandsman, we'd go to a performance site, after we'd eaten dinner, only to find food set up for us. Although we'd just eaten, this food was free, man! There are kids in Africa starving, how we could possibly waste free food. Luckily, most of our concerts were of a lighter vein. Hey, I'm trying to keep you awake here! The point is that diet is critical to physical fitness. Learn that before you have a heart attack and you'll be much better off.

Another part of physical fitness has to do with the amount of rest we get regularly. I remember a TV commercial that professed that "The best never rest!" Yeah, well, they die young. The body is not constructed to work 24/7 as we often think we can go. It needs to replenish its resources. There are myriad studies that conclude that if a person doesn't get enough rest he/she will break down psychologically as well as physically. I know there's not enough time to do all that you're asked to do, but if you don't rest, you'll eventually do nothing. Get plenty of rest and make sure your troops do the same...or else! The "or else" will manifest itself in illness, weakness, and fatigue, all of which lead to the inability to accomplish the mission. You know it's true.

One of the effects of maintaining physical fitness is that it affects our mental fitness. I recall that for most of my military life I was told, "We don't pay you to think, we pay you to do." Maybe, a hundred years ago (20 in military years), that might have been the case. Now, with technology changing our world on a daily basis, you and your troops have to think. Our military suffers in two areas, I think. One is that we don't think. The other is what we think about.

Imagine walking down the hallway of your duty section only to find a young troop sitting there, doing nothing. I mean, she's just sitting there. Doing nothing! Ha! I'm a Chief! I'll fix that! "Young lady, if you have nothing to do, let me find you something!" you say. Hey, I've been there! Done that! You feel much better, don't you? Well maybe you shouldn't. Is it possible that that young person was thinking?! Is it possible that she was this close to coming up with a better way to accomplish your mission? Is it possible? You'll never know now, will you? How is it we improve anything in our lives? Is it not through a thinking process? Someone, not you, thinks of a better way. Usually, it happens on the fly. Imagine if you and your troops made time to think of new ways to do things! As you mature (not age) you're going to find that the only way to remember anything is to write it down. Have you ever had a great idea and didn't write it down immediately? What happened? If you don't write it down, you will lose it! Have you ever come up with a new idea at work? When does it happen? Usually, while you're doing something, right? And you don't write it down, thinking you'll remember it. You know when you'll remember it? When someone else, who did write it down, comes up with it. "Hey, you know I thought of that before...." You tell your peers. Yeah, right!

The second thinking issue is what you think about. I tell you, if you don't get your troops to sit down and think about something specific, they'll think about everything else. Ever ask one of your troops, or yourself, "What were you thinking?" It's usually after they, or you, do something wrong that you ask that question. We do pay our troops to think. We have to! But we have to train them to do it!

Is the use of the mind, mental fitness, important? You know it is! So how do you exercise the mind? There are plenty of ways, but if you can't think of any, here are some suggestions. Reading! Leaders are readers! The problem with reading is that it takes time. None of us has time to read. We have to make time! You make time for watching Survivor, don't you? As with physical fitness, I'm not suggesting you read War and Peace. Make twenty minutes available each day to read books about your favorite subjects, your hobbies, or your work. You might find some peace of mind. You might even learn something. And the more you do it, the better you'll get at it. Read and learn.

One of the benefits many of my peers fought so hard for was tuition assistance. Now, as of this writing, 100 percent tuition assistance is available to every enlisted person on active duty. What a great benefit! Kudos to all of those who fought the fight and won! Again, I know none of you have time to go to school. Make time! But if you don't choose to do so, make sure you're troops do. You and I may have joined the Force as a patriotic gesture (Wait a minute. I have to be honest with you. I joined to dodge the draft. I do have some integrity.) but most young people now join up for the educational benefits. Now, like me, that purpose may, and I hope it does, evolve into a patriotic purpose, but the truth is that's not the reason most young folks are with you. How might that purpose evolve? By the way you lead them. Encourage your troops to go to school! Do all that you can to help them get there and they will return the favor in spades. Will going to school increase their mental abilities? Will that, in turn, help them think better? Given that you encourage thinking, will that not make your mission easier to accomplish? The answer to each of those questions is yes.

Physical fitness affects mental fitness. Both affect what we commonly call self-esteem. Someone once said that "what you see is what you'll be!" Confidence is maybe the most important thing a warrior must have when he or she is on the battle field. It comes from knowing your body and your mind are capable of any challenge. Self-confidence has a lot to do with emotional fitness. It affects the person as well as the team. It really is more about relationship fitness. And most of us have to relate with others on a daily basis. Is it important that we relate with each other? Only if you're a human being.

Who are you taking care of first? Take care of you, first! To develop emotional or relationship fitness, you have to start with you. I almost recall, about two centuries ago, the movie about Muhammad Ali titled The Greatest. Not the new version, but the real one. The theme song, sung by Whitney Houston, was The Greatest Love of All. The lyrics referred to the greatest love of all being the love for oneself. When I first heard it I thought, "how selfish." As I matured (not aged), I came to realize that loving oneself is the first step to emotional stability, or fitness. One cannot give what one does not have. (Wow, I hope I just made that up!) If you don't love yourself, how can you love anyone else? It's impossible! I hope you never have the experience of being around someone who's suicidal. A suicidal person has absolutely no love for themselves and they bring everyone around them down emotionally. You've been to those Suicide Prevention briefings every year. What they never get to is the real cause, and that's the lack of self-love. The only way to help those who don't love themselves is to love them until they do. That's not easy, but it's the truth.

Now, don't take me wrong. I'm not suggesting going to extremes, such as being egotist. But the ego must be strong for you to do what you have to do and that comes from self-confidence, self-esteem, self-love. Then you can share that love. In fact, I believe it happens almost naturally.

Okay, let's talk about the L word. I know it's touchy-feely, but the most important things in your life are touchy-feely, aren't they? What's most important to you? If you don't say "Family" you're probably reading this around your buds. I'll wait for you to be alone, then you'll say family. Isn't family synonymous with love? John and Paul were right, "All you need is love." Keep in mind there's a huge difference between love and lust. To put it in simple warrior terms, love is unconditional giving. Lust is selfish wanting. Easy enough?

Every relationship can be measured by the amount of love shared. Think about it. (Yes, now I'm asking you to practice what I preach.) The reason your relationship with another person is so strong is that you're willing to give him or her all you can, all you have. You're willing to give without the condition that he or she gives back to you. That's love! And there's incredible power in that! As I write this, my heart is saddened by the overwhelming number of our soldiers being killed in Iraq. Having been a warrior for all of my adult life, I know that the only way a soldier, Airman, sailor, marine, or coast guardsman can do what is expected is through the strength gained from love of country and fellow warrior. What can a person who puts his or her life on the line expect in return? Money? That's silly, isn't it? As a Chief, by now you must have come to the realization that you're in this not for the money or the prestige, but because you love what you do and who you do it for. It's about relationships. It's about love!

Interestingly, when you are physically, mentally, and emotionally fit, you find a sense of peace that empowers you to think beyond what's natural to the supernatural. That's spiritual fitness. Love is spiritual. Now, if you're getting antsy about this subject because you think I'm going to start preaching, don't! (Hey, I've been preaching all along! Amen!) Often, people misconstrue spirituality with religion. It's not necessarily the same. If religion is the way by which you develop spiritual fitness, then Halleluiah! If it's not, don't worry about it. To me, spiritually is about opening your mind and your heart to appreciate all that abounds around you.

I currently live in Colorado near Pike's Peak. Every morning I drive toward the west and get a glimpse of a giant post card. I see what Kathy Bates saw when she wrote the lyrics to America, the Beautiful. The mountains really are purple and they're majestic! Paradoxically, one of the most effective ways to get to the supernatural, the spiritual, is to appreciate the natural. Go outside, whether it's in the sunshine or the snow, and listen and observe. Hear the birds or the wind. Feel the breeze. Nature will astound you with its beauty if you pay attention.

Another way to develop your spirituality is by thinking (there I go again) about the value of the people you live and work with. Time has changed the risks of living in this world. There's a possibility, I hope not a probability, that all of those people you work with, live with, and, possibly, love, could get killed as you read this passage. God forbid that happen, but the possibility does exist. We are not as safe as we used to be. Imagine, again, God forbid, that your friends or family were all killed. How would you feel? Would that not put you in a spiritual frame of mind?

Surely, we don't know what we'd do if catastrophes like that befell us. But, in truth, we do know what we should do to express our appreciation and our love for those with whom we share our lives before a tragedy hits. We often choose not to. We choose not to because we don't exercise our spirit. You can change that. Today! Right now!

What I hope I've done in this lesson is to get you to complete a circle. Service before self begins with you, it goes out to others, and it comes back to you. Take care of yourself so that you can take care of others who, in turn, will take care of you.

War Story

This story is about developing oneself spiritually.

During my last assignment on active duty I served as Superintendent of the Support Group at Ramstein Air Base in Germany. Our building was situated in such a way that I could walk out of my office and see through my Lieutenant and see the DV hangar on the flightline. More often than I wish, I'd look out and notice a C-5, C-17, or C-130 taxiing to the hangar. The aircraft had to make some turns so it'd give me some time to think about what was right to do and to choose to do the right thing.

One of the things you can count on in Germany is that it will rain almost every day, unless it's snowing. If you don't know, know this. Chiefs do not cry! Sometimes our eyeballs sweat. The good thing about the weather in Germany is that when what I'm about to share with you occurred you couldn't tell whether it was the rain or my eyeballs sweating that created the rivers of moisture cutting along my face.

I'd stand in front of that DV hangar, at attention, while the cargo door of the respective aircraft was opened. I'd salute proudly as the "cargo" was prepared for deplaning. The "cargo" was flag-draped caskets. The Army calls this the Missing Soldier Ceremony. Regardless of what's it's called, it was a moment for me, and anyone there, usually the Base Honor Guard, to pay homage to our brothers and sisters in arms who expressed the last great measure of devotion, as President Abraham Lincoln called it, for you and for me to live in freedom. They gave their lives for us.

As I'd stand there, there were two emotions that swept through me. First was pride. I certainly never want any of my brothers and sisters in service to die but I know that each of us, when we sign up to be warriors, realizes that there's always a potential of death. Our loyalty to our country and to our fellow warrior overpowers any fear we may have and we go out and do what we're trained to do to accomplish the mission. I was, and still am, proud of those who were willing to die for what is right.

The other emotion was sorrow. Yes, I'd miss those men and women even if I'd never met them. I may not have known their personalities, but I knew their souls. The sorrow was in this thought: Somewhere in this world there's a little boy or a little girl whose Daddy or

Mommy is never coming home again. We warriors signed up for the risks involved in our profession of arms. The families don't. Our children, particularly when they're young, don't understand, and probably wouldn't accept, that their parents might die for the concept of freedom. Yet, so many kids have to live the rest of their lives missing their loved ones.

I've often said that the toughest job in military life is that of family member. When we go to war we take what we need most with us. When we go to war we leave what we love most to keep the fires burning. It takes a tremendous effort to stoke those fires.

I hope these thoughts have stoked a fire in you. You have to take care of yourself so that you can take care of your family and others. Some parts of fitness may be easier to maintain than others, but it takes a balance of all of them to be an effective servant-leader.

Let me close this lesson by telling you that I pray for you and for your families at least daily. I thank you for all you do and who you are. I thank your families for supporting you in your profession. Take care of them. But take care of yourself, first!

The 212-Degree Challenge

Am I physically fit?

- 211-degrees or less
- 212-degrees plus!

Am I mentally fit?

- 211-degrees or less
- 212-degrees plus!

How's my relationship with myself and with others?

- 211-degrees or less
- 212-degrees plus!

Am I spiritually fit?

- 211-degrees or less
- 212-degrees plus!

Bob Vásquez, CMSgt (Ret), USAF

Lesson 6

Acknowledge presence!

I once advised a group of troops to "Acknowledge presence!" and a young person (at my age, they're all young) called out, "You mean their gifts?" Being quick of wit, I immediately replied, "Yes! Exactly!" I enjoy playing with words. Especially homonyms. Yeah, I know, now you have to go look up the word. Presence. Presents. Is there a difference?

Have you ever been to a place of business and stood at the counter while the person who gets paid to serve you was talking to his girlfriend on the phone? He even saw you but continued his conversation at your expense. How'd that make you feel? Not so good, huh? When that has happened to me, I've walked out, never returned to that establishment, and told all of my friends about how I was treated. In the business sense, that's what's called customer service. Bad customer service! We often think about customer service in terms of an outsider coming to us to purchase a product or service. That's service for an external customer. The person we work for. There is another, equally important customer we often neglect, the internal customer, the person we serve with.

Do you think that that scenario I just described, where a person's mere existence isn't acknowledged, ever occurs at your unit? Maybe you haven't thought about it, so you can't answer the question. If you're part of a pretty good unit, it probably doesn't happen to your external customers. On the other hand, it may happen a lot more than you think to your internal customers. Here I go again, asking you to think!

One of the most effective things you can do as a servant-leader is to say "Good morning!" to your troops. Now, I'm assuming you have a day job. "Aw, man," you're saying, "that's such a piddley thing!" Yes! Exactly! It may be, however, the most important thing! What you're doing when you say "Good morning," or "Good afternoon" for you shift workers, is acknowledging presence. You're saying, "I know you're here!" Do it with a sincere smile and some enthusiasm and you're saying, "I know you're here and I'm glad you are!"

A word of caution - to do this right, you have to care. You have to be humble. You can't fake it. If you don't care, just going through the motions, they'll see right through you. You may have heard the adage, "People don't care how much you know, they want to know how much you care." The truth is that they always know how much you care by how you act. Here's an example.

I don't like saying negative things about people, but a paradigm was validated for me when I met President Jimmy Carter. He was known as the Smiling President. He was internationally known for his broad grin. Many said it was fake. I, literally, went out of my way to attend his Bible Study at his church in Plains, Georgia one summer. What a brilliant man! When I introduced myself to him, however, and told him I was an active duty Chief Master Sergeant serving overseas, he just smiled and said, "Congratulations!" and moved on. I could sense that he really wasn't interested. Luckily, he shook my hand. In other words, he really didn't acknowledge my presence. He looked at me but never really saw me. You can imagine my disappointment. Your troops always see right through you. Whether you're the

President of the United States, the Queen, or *THE* Chief, what you feel will be expressed in your words and deeds. You can't help it. Or maybe you can!

Saying "Good morning!" to someone may be the most powerful thing you can do all day for that person. It sets the tone for the rest of the day, depending on how you say it. If your troops are geographically separated from you and you make it a point to seek them out to acknowledge their presence they will remember it. And they will appreciate it, even if they don't tell you so. While I was on active duty, I was always amazed at how my just showing up to a unit was seen as a great event. Not that I was great or shared any sage advice with them. Just my being there told them I cared and they appreciated it. A very small thing to do indeed, but the impact was profound. Even now, I'll see troops that I was stationed with who will remind me that I visited their unit. I acknowledged their presence and they still remember.

This lesson works with your boss as well. Acknowledging the boss's presence goes a long way in developing trust. It's been my experience that the higher you move up the ladder of success, the less your value is acknowledged on a daily basis. You're expected to produce and often are taken for granted. That's just a natural business process, I think. We all want to be valued and enjoy when others express their appreciation for our service. If that's true, doesn't it make sense that acknowledging the boss's value would be a good thing in developing or maintaining the relationship?

Remember what I said about the boss's vision being your mission? We all need a pat on the back. A sincere, "Good morning!" will provide that. The investment is minimal compared to the return. Find your boss every morning and acknowledge her presence. It will work wonders in how you both work together toward a common goal.

By the way, a homonym is a word that sounds like another word but has a different meaning. Feel better now? Earlier I wrote: "Presence. Presents. Is there a difference?" There is, obviously, in how the two words are defined. But the concepts of both go together in the context of being *THE* Chief. What is your most important resource when trying to accomplish a mission? Isn't it your people? Yeah, you need equipment, but nothing's going to get done without the right people doing what they know how to do. Every one of your troops has been blessed with specific talents. Those talents are gifts. The gifts they have to share, and they themselves, are presents! Acknowledge that! Acknowledge your troops! Acknowledge their presents!

What can you do by yourself? Don't you need the folks you work with? More now than before is my guess. Don't you appreciate them? Surely, you do! Show them! Every day! Say "Good morning!" "Good afternoon!" Ask about their family. It's the most important thing in the world to them, just like it is to you. Acknowledge their presence. They truly are a gift! Your troops, your bosses, all have different functions, but they're all worth the same: Everything!

War Story

I had the honor of meeting President Ronald Reagan back in 1993. I was assigned to the 15th Air Force Band, stationed at March Air Force Base, California. The Band had performed several times for the President while he was in office so after he retired in the Los Angeles area he asked us to come to his office so that he could thank us. He wanted to acknowledge our presents. (Yes, that's a homonym.) Now, think on that a little bit. A former President of the United States summoning an Air Force Band to his office to thank them! That, my friends, is acknowledging presence in a big way!

We took advantage of the invitation and went to his office one bright sunny day (It's always bright and sunny in California!). What an exciting time! The President invested more than an hour with us, joking around and telling stories. What a great storyteller! We all got our pictures taken with him (I have mine proudly displayed in my office if you'd like to come by and see it.). His next appointment, evidently, was some golf tournament. He was dressed casually, obviously having to get to the course right after talking with us. I was the second to the last person to be photographed with the President. My commander was last. I'd trained him right. As we finished taking the photos, one of the President's aides came in and admonished him that he needed to hurry to get to his next commitment. The President acknowledged what the aide said but finished taking the photos. He could have apologized and gone off to do what his aide was rushing him to do, but, instead, he stayed with us until we were all done.

I'd taken my book, Ronald Reagan: *An American Life*, the President's autobiography, with me to get his autograph. We hadn't had time to get to that so as we were being led out of his office I asked another aide at a desk near the door we were going out of if she would please ask the President to autograph my book and I would gladly leave enough money with her to cover the postage to mail it to me. The President was being escorted out another door, but he stopped. Evidently, he'd overheard my conversation with the aide at the desk. He stopped, told the aide with him to get my book, signed it, had his aide return it to me, and then went on his way.

Did he have to do that? Of course not! But he did! He cared enough to stop what he was doing to take care of someone he didn't know very well but respected. He even remembered my name, and, most importantly, my rank. He signed it,

To Chief Bob Vasquez - With Best Wishes.

Ronald Reagan

May 17-'93

You're welcome to come see my book as well. I won't let you touch it, but you can see it.

Many people loved President Reagan. Even more respected him. Surely, history will remember what he did for the country, but the people he touched will always remember him for how he treated them. I would have gone to war with him any time, any place!

I've recently had the honored of working with a retired general, Major General (Retired) Gary Dylewski, who was one of President Reagan's military aides while the President was still in office. I've told General Dylewski this story several times, and each time he tells me that that was the way the President was. He'd acknowledge Margaret Thatcher's presence as easily as he would the White House janitor he'd see along the way to meeting the world's heads of state. And he made each feel as though they were a great gift to democracy.

On 17 May, 1993, President Ronald Reagan, the Great Communicator, took the time to acknowledge my value, my presence, by stopping in his tracks, en route to an important event, to sign my book. He even called me, "Chief!" I will forever acknowledge his presents! He was a gift! He was a great servant-leader! He was *THE* Chief!

The 212-Degree Challenge

Do I appreciate my troops?

- 211-degrees or less

- 212-degrees plus!!

Do I acknowledge my troops' presence (and presents) every day?

- 211-degrees or less

- 212-degrees plus!

Do I redirect my troops when they get off track?

- 211-degrees or less

- 212-degrees plus!

Do I acknowledge my commander's presence?

- 211-degrees or less

- 212-degrees plus!

Bob Vásquez, CMSgt (Ret), USAF

Lesson 7

Just say no!

Those of you who were around during the Reagan administration may recall Nancy Reagan's anti-drug campaign for teens called "Just Say No!" That's not what I'm referring to in this lesson. Wait a minute! Maybe it is...in a way.

This lesson is on work versus family. Let me start with some thoughts on work because that's probably what you'd do if I asked you to say something about each. In fact, you're reading this book to help you at work, right? Read deeper, it might help you with your family life as well.

Work often becomes addictive. You don't even realize it. You may be one of those who can hardly wait to get to your computer to see all those e-mails someone stayed up all night writing and sending to you to make your day. You may be one of those folks who complain about the excessive number of e-mails you get every day. But you sit at your desk all day, watching with great anticipation, as they come up. You may even get perturbed when you don't get an e-mail for more than thirty minutes. You even check your computer's connections to make sure everything is intact! "No e-mails? Man, the server must be down."

If I asked you to choose what's most important to you, work or family, there's an extremely high probability that you'd choose family. Yet, if I follow up with asking you where you spend most of your time, you'll probably answer, "at work, or working." What's up with that? How can family be more important to you yet you spend most of your time working? Oh yes, I know your argument! You work to support your family. That's partly true. By the time you make Chief, however, you work because you enjoy it. You could have quit a long time back, but you didn't. Okay, those of you who made E-9 in five years can't quit yet, but you get my drift.

You're still working! The truth is, your work defines you. Ever meet someone at the airport for the first time? How do you introduce yourself? You give the person your name immediately followed by what you do for a living. You certainly don't mention your family background until after a few drinks.

Your work defines you. Why do we work so hard or so much? Because it's easy! "Wait a minute," you say, "My work is tough!" You want tough? Try raising a family! That's tough! Let me tell you why you spend most of your time at work, the real reason. Again, it's easy! At work you know the rules. You know when you're supposed to be there. You know what to do. You know how to address people. In fact, you were trained to do what you do at work. Now, how much training did you get to be a parent or a spouse? That's tough! The rules are made up as you go along, usually not by you, and they get tougher as time goes by.

At work you can tell your Airmen, what and when to do what you want them to do and they'll do it. Or you can put them in jail! Okay, you can recommend they go to jail. The commander will probably take your recommendation. What do you do when your teenager doesn't do what you tell her? Put her in jail? Watch out! She may send you to jail for child abuse.

At work you have all, or most, of the resources you need to accomplish your mission. Oh, you'll complain about not having this or that, it's your nature. I don't know anyone who has anywhere near all the resources they need at home. Whether it's time, money, or things, we never seem to be able to quite have what we need to give our families what they want.

Work is fun! Come on, be honest! If it weren't fun, you'd have gotten out a long time ago. Yes, you have a lot of responsibilities, but you also have a lot more help than you do at home.

Do you see the connection with Mrs. Reagan's campaign? Work is addictive and it affects your teens and your spouses, your families. Here's the lesson.

Remember when I talked about taking care of yourself first and that I mentioned the Core Value of Service Before Self? Sometimes you have to just say no to work and go home to the family. That's integrity, doing what's right.

Because your work defines you, you'll probably find it very difficult to just say no. Since you're now a Chief and, subsequently, don't have anything to do but walk around with a coffee cup in your hand talking to people, you'll be asked to do a lot more than you should. It will be fun stuff to do so you'll want to say yes to all of those requests! You'll be asked to speak here and there for this and that, to serve on this panel or that board. All kinds of fun things! Hey, you've got nothing else to do, right? Of course, I'm being facetious. You've got plenty to do, but now your new notoriety makes you a target for even more! Hey, you're a Chief, you can handle it! But can your family?

Here's a slide I use in one of my Time Management seminars that, I think, puts it in perspective.

- Because we don't know what is really important to us, everything seems important.
- Other people, unfortunately, see us doing everything, so they expect us to do everything.
- Doing everything keeps us so busy, we don't have time to think about what's really important to us.

Integrity first! You're going to have to shut the door and take care of your family every once in a while or you will lose them. If you have kids, don't blink because when you open your eyes they will have grown into people. You'll wonder what happened and the answer is that while you were busy saying yes to your work, they kept on growing and left you behind.

Now, one of your arguments will be that the boss expects you to say yes when she asks you to do more than you expected on the day that your first-born son has his first ballet recital. How do we make decisions? How do leaders, even yours, make decision? Isn't it always based on the information they have. Do you get up in the morning thinking, "Hmmm...what can I really screw up today?" No! Neither does your boss.

Every leader wants to be a good leader, otherwise they're really not a leader. She wants to make good decisions. Help her. Give her all of the data she needs to make the right decisions. In other words, if your boss doesn't know your son is about to graduate from ballet academy how is she going to know not to ask you to stay later? Everyone, unanimously, says that family is the most important part of their lives. And if you've developed any kind of respectful relationship with your boss she won't keep you from meeting your family commitments. As long as she knows they exist! Tell her what's most important, then both of you can just say no to the work. It'll still be there tomorrow, trust me.

Work, like drugs, can, and will, become addictive, especially as a Chief, because there's so much of a payback for doing good things for others. Follow Nancy Reagan's advice and just say no! Do what's right for you and your family as well as for the Force. That will mean going home when you should. Not taking that TDY that seems like it will be so much fun. Not going to that function when your son or daughter is graduating from karate school. It also means taking time for yourself. You can't stop growing. An effective servant-leader ensures she grows on the inside as well as on the outside. (I'm not talking about physical growth here. That will come on its own.) It's tough, but so are you! I know that you want to be *THE* Chief at work. You can do that, but that's temporary.

You'll always be Dad or Mom. Servant-leadership is about doing what's right at work and at home. You have to strike the balance, which is almost never 50-50, between your work and your family. It will always be easier to say no to your family. Take courage! When someone asks you to do one more fun thing at work and you know your family is counting on you to be with them at the same time, just say no to the work. You won't regret it in the long term. Trust me!

War Story

Man, I was so proud of myself! It was about noon when I got home and as I walked in the house I found my lovely-bride-of-16-wonderful-and-fulfilling-years, Deb, and my 10-year-old daughter, Tesa, having a discussion. Okay, they were arguing. Oh, all right, they were fighting! I didn't know, nor did I really care, what they were fussing about. I had a very important announcement to make!

I quieted them down and proudly announced that I had just been selected to be the Commandant of the March Air Force Base Noncommissioned Officer Academy. Hey, this was such an historic event I left work two hours early! I gave up my daily tee time to go home to share my excitement with my family! I'd worked so hard to reach that pinnacle of success! No other bandsman had ever done that! "Man, I'm good!" I thought. "I've made it to the top!"

As I expected, I could see the pride in Deb's green eyes. Tesa, our first-born, looked at me as intently as I'd ever seen her look, and without a moment's hesitation said, "Fine, Dad, now will you help me pick up poop?" As you may imagine, my ego immediately deflated to nothing.

You see, although my career was of the highest importance to me, what was much more important to Tesa was what I often considered minutiae. It's the little things that our children and our families find important. Often, our children won't know, nor care, what we do as a profession, but they'll always know whether we were there when they needed us. And they will always remember.

I did go out and help Tesa pick up poop. Afterward we sat down on the stoop and she said to me, without any prompting, "Dad, I'm proud of you." I never asked her if she was referring to my news or my help. It didn't matter. She was proud of me and that's all that mattered that day.

Here's the moral. Pay attention to what your family needs and be there for them. It may be difficult, but just say no to work and yes to family more than you have in the past. It doesn't matter how often you've already done it, it hasn't been enough. One day you'll retire and the folks you invested the majority of your life with will forget you. Oh, not totally, especially if you were an effective servant-leader. New folks will come into the unit. They will have heard of you, but they won't know you. Eventually, those folks won't even know you as a Chief. Your family, on the other hand, will never forget you. And you'll always be Mom or Dad or Honey to them. Will they call you that with a capital or in the lower case?

Being *THE* Chief is great, but being Dad, or Mom, or Honey, is greater! The way I assess whether or not I've accomplished my mission as a father is in this way: When I look into my girls' eyes, and that includes Deb, and say, "I love you, Baby!" And they look back at me and say, "I know!" then I've done my duty.

The 212-Degree Challenge

Do I say no to the good so that I can say yes to the best?

- 211-degrees or less

- 212-degrees plus!

Do I know what my highest values really are?

- 211-degrees or less

- 212-degrees plus!

Do I live up to what I say is most important?

- 211-degrees or less

- 212-degrees plus!

Do I know what is truly important to my troops and my commander?

- 211-degrees or less

- 212-degrees plus!

Bob Vásquez, CMSgt (Ret), USAF

Lesson 8

Build trust!

Trust is the glue that binds a relationship. Without it everything will, literally, fall apart. You're in a life-or-death business. Can you do anything totally by yourself? (I asked that question before, didn't I?) Of course not! Aren't you more comfortable, more confident, when you know someone is there to "check your six?" Unless things have changed drastically in the last few days, you probably have just enough people on your work team to get the job done.

The truth is you don't have enough; you just make do with who you've got. That means that you need everyone on the team to do their part and you have to trust that they will. To build trust, you have to build relationships. Your effectiveness as a servant-leader is measured by the strength of your relationships with your co-workers. If you, and the people you serve, are going to be effective, you have to trust each other.

How do you build trust? If I asked you to define trust, chances are you'd say something like, "It's when someone is always honest." How about, "When people do what they say they're going to do, you trust them." Or, "When you know you can count on her, you trust her." Those are all good thoughts but the problem with them is that they refer to what others do. Trust begins with your own thoughts and deeds. If I already shared this thought with you it bears repeating. Dr Stephen Covey says that everything is created twice - first in the mind, then in the physical sense. In order to build trust in a relationship, you have to be trustworthy. You have to think about what's right, then you have to do it. Remember the adage, "If it is to be, it is up to me!"

Let me back up a little bit. Who do we trust? I've compiled a list of eight criteria that answers that question. If you're going to build trust, however, you're going to have to fit these criteria. I'm not sure it's an exhaustive list, but it will get you started. Let me share that list and explain each, then I'll get back to the point I'm trying to make.

1. We trust people who are competent.

One of the worst things you can do as a leader is to try to snow your troops into thinking you know more than you do. I won't preach on Lesson 2, but it's important to know what you know and what you don't know. Remember that you're a Chief, not a super-grade technician. You're a leader and that's what you have to be competent at. As the great philosopher, Dirty Harry, once said, "A man's gotta know his limitations." Trust is a two way street, however, so you'll have to figure out what you need to know at the level you're at and show your troops that you're willing to empower them to make decisions based on their expertise. Be aware, though, that if you're going to trust in their competence, and you should, you're going to have to ensure they're trained and experienced.

I recently had an old guy's "procedure" done. A "procedure." Yeah, right! Why do the medics try to confuse us? The doc stuck a foreign object into me and used it to cut stuff out! Just tell me the truth! It's like going to have "labs done." Man, they're going to suck out your blood! Okay, enough on that. The point is that we trust people who are competent. When the doc and I talked about the "procedure," my first question was, "Have you done this before?" "About 25,000 times," he answered. "In fact, I'm a national spokesperson for the value of men your age having this done." I felt much better. Imagine if he'd answered, "No this is my first time, as it is yours, but we should be okay, I've read the manual." No, man! I want only a competent person cutting into me. I put my complete trust in that doc's competence and I lived to write about it.

2. We trust people who are confident.

Imagine that doc answering my question about how often he'd done that "procedure" by saying, "Well, Chief, I've never actually done it, and, to be honest, I'm scared to do it." Man, I would have walked out of his office as quickly as my old legs could travel! You may remember a scene in a movie titled U-571 in which a young Lieutenant Tyler (Matthew McConaughey) becomes the submarine's skipper by default after the commander is killed. The Lieutenant isn't doing too good a job at leading his men. Over a cup of coffee, Harvey Keitel, playing the Chief, asks the lieutenant for permission to "speak freely." The skipper, of course, grants him permission. The Chief admonishes him, saying, "The commanding officer is a mighty and terrible thing, a man to be feared and respected. All-knowing. All-powerful. The skipper always knows what to do whether he does or not." What the Chief was trying to tell the skipper is that followers trust leaders who are confident and decisive. No decision is a decision. As a leader you'll probably make a few bad decisions, but you have to be confident in making your decisions. As I said in the previous lesson, leaders make decisions based on the information they have. Get the information you need then make a confident decision. People will trust you when you do.

3. We trust people who keep us informed.

You've heard the adage that "information is power." That's bunk! Information can't think! People think! Sometimes…. Information doesn't care about power, it's just information. Shared information is powerful! The dictionary defines power as "the capacity to act effectively." Does information itself have capacity? No! People do! Power lies in people and how they perform. Power is increased when information is shared. Once again, how do you, as a leader, make decisions? It's based on the information you have at hand. If you don't have all of the valid information you need, you'll end up making bad decisions. You trust, or should trust, the people who keep you informed, especially those who provide you the bad news. Every colonel and general officer I ever worked with admonished me to keep them informed, especially of the bad news. Every one of them chartered me to keep them out of trouble by telling them when their decision might be a bad one based on the information I had. They knew I'd have different information than they were given.

I remember General John Jumper, then Commander of the United States Air Forces in Europe, asking the USAFE Band to develop a tattoo for Ramstein Air Base to be performed on the Air Force's birthday, in September. A tattoo is a military ceremony, usually done in the evening, with music and marching. It's a very exciting and interesting ceremony. This was a very high-level event, especially since the Big Boss had personally asked for it and many other Big Bosses were expected to attend. You can imagine the amount of effort it took to coordinate everything.

After months of work, we were notified to ensure we had a rain plan because the weather folks expected rain on the day the tattoo was scheduled for. Duh! It always rains all of September in Germany! Anyway, we thought we had that in the plan. The performance day arrived and, lo and behold, we awoke to constant showers. The weather guys were right for once! Panic, everyone! The sky is falling! Literally! As soon as I got to work I got the call to get to a meeting to work out what we were going to do. The rain plan called for taking the tattoo indoors. Not a problem, you'd think...if you've never been stationed at Ramstein. Ramstein has to be the busiest base in the world. Okay, you think what you want, but it's the truth. The hangar we'd planned on using in case of rain, back a few months ago when we developed the plan, now had a C-130 parked in it. In pieces. I know, your first thought is to move it out. No can do! Like Humpty Dumpty, all of the general's men couldn't put it together again in time to move it out and prepare the hangar for the tattoo.

Aha! There are other hangars on that base. Let's use another! The others, too, weren't available. After much cussing and discussing, someone suggested we get in touch with the Logistics Group Commander to find us a hangar. Hey, at least we could then blame him for not making it happen and we'd be clear. The LG told us none were available. Someone at the table said something about going by Hangar 3 and having seen it empty. We called the LG back and told him what we'd heard. Nope. It's got airplane pieces in it. It was about lunch time now, so we decided to take a break and return in an hour.

Being the sly and cunning enlisted guy that I was, I decided to stop by Hangar 3 to check it out and maybe come up with other options. As I walked into the hangar a Master Sergeant came up to greet me. He was smiling a huge smile because I'd come by. (Remember Lesson 6, Acknowledge Presence!?) After some chit-chat, I asked him if he was expecting to get some gear in because the hangar looked empty to me. He said, "No, Chief, we just cleared it out." You know what I did. I called my boss so that he could get the credit for fixing the problem. Hey, what was I shooting for, E-10? (My boss did get promoted that cycle, by the way.)

We did the gig and it went tremendously well in spite of the weather. The point is that the LG, who was a great leader in his own right, made his decisions based on the information he had. The Master Sergeant hadn't had time to tell anyone his crew had completed its task way ahead of time. He had the information but hadn't shared it yet. Sharing information is powerful! It provides us the capacity to act effectively. I think you'll agree that we trust those who keep us informed.

4. We trust people who listen to us.

I already gave you the lesson on listening. That was in Lesson 2. Let me reiterate, however, how important listening is to the communication process. I think you can just about conclude that every problem we ever face ends up being a problem with communication. I've got a couple of pieces of paper hanging on my wall that prove I know something. I'm not sure how valid those papers are, but I do know that every communications class I ever took dealt with developing skills to better express myself. Obviously, that's important. I've never taken a college course, however, that focused on developing my listening skills. It's like work and family. Work is easy. Talking is easy. Raising a family is difficult. Listening is difficult. In my communication talks, I usually make the distinction between expression and impression. Expression is when we try to make someone else think we know something. Impression is when we open our ears, our eyes, and hearts so that we can learn something about someone else.

We trust good listeners who are sincere about being empathic, not judgmental, and are just willing to be there for us. I recall a story Leo Buscaglia tells about a four-year old child whose next-door neighbor was an elderly gentleman who had recently lost his wife. Upon seeing the man cry, the little boy went into the old gentleman's yard, climbed onto his lap, and just sat there. When his mother asked him what he had said to the neighbor, the little boy said, "Nothing, I just helped him cry." Sometimes it takes a four-year old to teach us older folk's important lessons. Most four-year olds haven't developed the biases we "mature" folks have. They can listen without passing judgment. We should learn to listen like they do.

5. We trust people who are considerate, who care.

I've invested weeks of energy contemplating whether being considerate and being caring are the same or not. They're so similar that I combine them here. I believe that a caring person is considerate, thus consideration is a byproduct of caring. You can argue with me and I'd enjoy it. I'll look forward to hearing from you. Milton Mayeroff writes in his book, On Caring, that caring "is to help [another person] grow and actualize himself." Caring, like listening, requires the carer to be empathic, not to pass judgment. Remember I quoted Dr Stephen Covey saying that everything is created twice? Caring starts with the will to care. You have to want to do it. The will comes from a thought to care but you wouldn't have thought it if it wasn't in your heart to begin with. Yeah, it's a circle. Life is a circle. A caring person can make life so much better!

If you care about your troops, you'll be considerate of them. It's like service before self. You'll think of the consequences your actions, your words, and your thoughts might have on someone's life. Being considerate isn't just doing unto others as you would have them do unto you, it's doing unto others as they would like you to do for them. It takes visual listening. You have to pay attention to their needs and act accordingly. As the great philosopher, Yogi Berra said, "You can observe a lot by watching." If you're truly interested in your troops' growth, you'll work on being considerate and helping them actualizes themselves.

Refer back to Lesson 6 again. Acknowledge presence. As I said in that lesson, one of the most powerful ways you'll show people you care is by searching them out and saying "Good morning!" It's a small price to pay for a huge return on investment. It shows you care.

6. We trust people who make themselves available.

I know of a leader who tells his troops that he has an open door policy yet when the troops try to make an appointment to see him, he's never there. As difficult as it may be for you to make time to be with your people, you'll have to make time to be an effective servant-leader. When you tell your troops you'll be there, be there. No excuses. That may mean just saying no to your boss, but make sure your boss knows your intent is to develop trust with your troops and that it will be a priority. Or fail. It's always your choice.

Here's a lesson I learned the hard way. As most of us do now, instead of saying "Good morning" or "good afternoon" we say, "How's it going?" Don't ask that unless you're truly interested. I'm still working on breaking that habit. Here's why. As a Chief, you'll be fairly well known if for no other reason than you wear those stripes that cover up most of your upper arm. I was always fairly well known at every base I was stationed at, sometimes to my detriment. I'd walk around asking people, "How are you doing?" Often, they'd stop me to tell me! Oh, it wasn't so bad if I had the time, but if I was in a hurry to get somewhere, I had to make a tough call on what, or who, was more important. I learned to leave really early for my appointments away from where I worked, just in case

I was stopped. It was the only way I could assure my troops I was available when they needed me. They always seem to need you when you're walking down the street. Stop for them. Make yourself available.

7. We trust people who are consistent.

Maybe not consistently bad or wrong, although at least you can count on that and do what you need to do about it. I think proactively, so what I mean is that we trust those who are always there for us and always do their best. They're the ones who you can count on to "have your back." One of my favorite TV characters was Radar O'Reilly, on M.A.S.H.. Every time the colonel even thought of something he needed, Radar was standing next to him, having accomplished it. Man, was he consistent!

Again, recall Lesson 6, Acknowledge presence!. I suggested you go find your troops and wish them good morning or good afternoon. You have to be consistent. You can't do it just once and think that its effect will last forever. No, wait a minute. If you do it just once the effect will last forever. They will always remember. If you do it every time you can, especially if it's every day, you'll make a huge impact. They'll always remember that too.

You have to be consistent on the positive side. It'll build trust.

8. Lastly, we trust people who are principle-centered.

One of the things we've struggled with for as long as we've been a force is the issue of loyalty. We want our troops to be loyal, but loyal to what, or should I say whom? Is it more important for our troops to follow us or to do what's right, especially when we're wrong? The right answer is for them to do what's right, not only what we expect. Being principle-centered, I think, is the true test of our leadership and our professionalism.

What principles should we be loyal to? Without getting into semantics, I think we can accept the Air Force Core Values as the principles to live up to. How can we fail if we do what's right in a selfless manner in everything we do all the time? Would you not trust someone who could live up to that standard? Of course you would!

Now, those are the people we trust. Building trust, however, is an inside-out process. As I said at the start of this lesson, you have to be trustworthy to even begin to build trust. You have to do the eight things I just shared with you. And you have to do them all, all of the time! Doing only one is not going to produce trust. It's an all-or-nothing proposition here. That doesn't mean you can't work on one area, especially if you're deficient in that area, it just means that to truly build trust you'll have to work on developing a balance of the eight areas. It may take work, but you can do it.

An old professor of mine, Dr Don Hardisty, used to say, "Life is simple once you understand its complexities." I've just shared the complexities of trust with you, the simple part is that you can affect them just by doing them every day. And the more you do them, the more trustworthy you'll be. Work on you, first, then you can lead them! Trust me! You'll be glad you did.

War Story

"Sergeant Vasquez (I was a SMSgt at the time.), you've got to do something about this guy!" I'm not sure this was the first thing I heard as I arrived to my new band assignment, but it's what I remember hearing first. I was fairly new to leading and I was anxious to do it right. "What do I need to do?" I asked. "Get rid of him," was the advise I was given.

Now, I'd been through Leadership School and the NCO Academy so I wasn't totally ignorant. I figured the first thing I should do was to investigate whether what I was being told was true. "What's wrong with him?" I asked. "All he does is sit in his office reading his Bible," was the answer. "Really?" I thought. "Hmmm...."

His office was along my way to the rehearsal room so I made it a point to see what he was doing. Amazingly, every day I passed by, all I saw him doing was sitting at his desk reading a book. Finally, I stopped and talked with him.

"Good morning!" I said.

"Good morning, Sir," he responded, respectfully.

"I'm new here and I'm trying to get to know everyone and what they do. What is your AFSC?"

"I'm a vocalist, Sir."

"Oh? A singer, huh? I haven't heard you sing. Which group do you sing with?"

"I don't, Sir."

"You don't? What do you do?"

"I sit here and read my Bible."

"You do? That's all you do?"

"Yes, Sir."

"Why is that all you do?"

"Because I was told to."

"You were told to sit here and read your Bible and not sing with any group even though you're a singer?"

"Yes, Sir, that's right."

"Can you sing?"

"Yes, Sir, I love to sing?'

"Okay, here's what we're going to do. Find me some songs that you'd like to sing with the big group. Bring me a tape of three or four and I'll arrange them for you and we'll see how well you do. Don't rush. We'll get to them as soon as possible, though. How does that sound?"

You may have heard people say a person's eyes sparkle. I can't describe this young person's sparkling eyes and the huge smile he drew across his face. He was, literally, beaming. "Thank you, Sir!" he said and I went on my way.

First thing next morning he was at my door with a tape in hand. I was surprised, but grateful for his initiative. He'd done his part, now I had to do mine. I worked diligently to arrange the tunes he wanted to do as quickly as I could. Within a few days they were ready and I made sure to schedule time to try them. He could sing! In fact, he blew the walls down!

I never dug deep enough to find out why he hadn't been given a chance before I got there, but it didn't matter much to me. My sense is that they didn't trust him for some reason. I gave him my full trust. We had several singers in the big group. Since he was the ranking person, I made him the lead singer and put him in charge of preparing the other singers so that I could invest my time with the instrumentalists and write more. He was one of the best leaders I ever knew. He went on to other assignments, eventually being STEP promoted, served as an Additional Duty First Sergeant and Operations NCO, he was a gifted man who excelled once given the opportunity and freedom.

This young man taught me a lot about building trust. He wasn't perfect, but who is? I made sure I lived up to those eight tenets I shared with you to enable him to be his best, to flourish. And it worked. We still have a great relationship and he knows that if he ever needs me, I'm there. And I know I can always trust in him if I need him. Trust is the glue. If you build it, they will come!

The 212-Degree Challenge

Do I trust my troops and my commander?

- 211-degrees or less

- 212-degrees plus!

Am I trustworthy?

- 211-degrees or less

- 212-degrees plus!

Do I continuously work on building trust in my relationships?

- 211-degrees or less

- 212-degrees plus!

Do I ensure everyone within my unit works on being trustworthy?

- 211-degrees or less

- 212-degrees plus!

Lesson 9

Gratitude is everything!

You've heard that attitude is everything, and there is a lot of truth in that, but I think that the deeper truth is that one of the things we don't do often enough is to think about the many blessings we, as Americans, enjoy. Too often, we take those blessings for granted. To be an effective servant-leader, you have to make time to think about what you have. It's easy to think about what you don't have. Be grateful. You're blessed!

Think about the freedom you enjoy. People often complain about getting old. One of the best things about getting older is that, as my mentor, Dr Tom Boyd, tells me, you figure out what's important to do and you don't do what's not. You will, I hope, get to a point in your life, and maybe you're there now, when you can do what you

147

want to do, when you want to do it and don't have to ask permission. That goes with acknowledging the many freedoms we enjoy. Having lived in Europe for many years, one of the pains of traveling there is that you have to carry a passport wherever you go. Don't get me wrong, it's worth the effort, and I think it's neat to be able to experience the diverse cultures each country has, but here in America, you can just pick up and go wherever you want, whenever you want, as long as you can afford the gas, of course.

There are few countries where you can say whatever you want even, or should I say, especially, about government leaders without getting in trouble. The U.S. media is free to print anything they want. If you're naïve enough you can believe what it prints. That's freedom! I've been in countries where if you looked at a woman, not necessarily in a sexual manner, you could lose a part of your anatomy! I don't mean to diss anyone's culture. My point is that there is no other country in the entire world where people enjoy all the freedoms Americans do. You are an American! Be grateful for that! Daily!

As an American, you're a target for many people who can't understand the concept of freedom and are bent on destroying that concept at all costs. Develop the Gratitude Attitude by considering how important your bosses, troops, and family are. First, remember they're people, just like you. They have the same basic needs, but they also have different needs than yours. I recall counseling one of my favorite commanders, Col Denny Layendecker, on this particular subject. He is, truly, a genius. As such, his expectations of his people were very high and he'd often become aggravated when they didn't reach their potential.

We'd sit in his office and I'd listen to him vent until he'd ask for my advice. "Sir," I'd ask him, "what if all of your troops got on a bus (which is an event that occurred quite regularly) and as they drove down the highway, a bomb exploded in it, killing or maiming every one of them?" Unfortunately, that's a risk that troops the world over now take on a daily basis. "How would you feel?" I'd ask him. The good colonel would become teary-eyed and answer, "It would break my heart, Chief." "Well, think about it, Sir. What I just described could happen, although I hope it won't. I know you care about those troops and that you only want them to do their best, but doing doesn't compare to being." I'd somehow convince him that he should be grateful to be in command of such great folks. Yes, they all had to grow, but so do we.

As I'd try to convince the colonel to appreciate his troops I tried to inspire the troops to appreciate the colonel's talents and caring. "We're all in this together," I'd admonish them. "We should all appreciate each other. We will, one day, so why not make that day today?" The Gratitude Attitude will always take us a long way.

All of my military life I've dealt with change, some of it positive and some of it just plain stupid. Much of that change was top driven. What I learned was that whatever changed today would probably change again in a couple of years when the commander moved on. The problem is that you never knew whether the new commander would be better or worse. Luckily, for me, I had the opportunity to work with the best and the worst! Most were the best. As I grew up and opened my eyes, I realized that the commander has a lot of responsibility and very little time to do what is expected. I learned to value each commander for the good things he or she did for the troops and forgive the failures. As Zig Ziglar says, "Failure is an event, not a person."

I also realized that leaders make decisions based on the information they have at hand. I figured out that when I kept the boss informed, she could make better decisions. The point here is that commanders are people too. Everyone has different ways of leading. Learn to appreciate those you're bound, by law, to follow. Do you remember my question about your first thought in the morning being, "What can I really screw up today?" Your troops don't think that, you don't think that, and your boss doesn't think that. Things just happen sometimes that no one can control. Be grateful for those commanders who try. Your troops will learn to appreciate their leader, you, by the way you appreciate your leader.

That's work-related gratitude. The most important part of your life, surely, is your family. We don't thank our families enough. And there's little we can do to express the real gratitude most of us feel for those people who stick with us for 20 or 30 years. I firmly believe we should have a national holiday honoring the military family. Time magazine's 2003 "Person of the Year" was the American soldier. Rightfully so. This year's honor should go to the families who suffer as much, if not more, than the warriors they support. Think about that.

When a military unit deploys, what do the troops take with them? Everything! Oh, it's not quite the enmities of home, but they take food, water, medics, communications equipment, transportation, and everything else they'll need to accomplish the mission, not to mention weapons. What is the spouse left with? Little to nothing! I can't tell you how often a spouse would come into our Family Support Center at Ramstein Air Base Germany without any money to feed her family. The spouse, who managed the finances had been deployed on short notice and didn't think about his family, so now they're in deep hurt. Now, I know that *THE* Chief won't let that happen in her unit, but it does happen in others.

Talk about draw downs! When a military person deploys the family unit's manning is cut by 50% and the mission requirements of the remaining person is increased by 100%. Imagine that happening at your unit! You'd have a fit! Yet the military spouse goes through that as often as you deploy. And as I said earlier, it's fun...for you! Our spouses just put up with it...if we're lucky.

Be grateful for your spouse and kids who probably endure a lot more than you as you fulfill your destiny to maintain the freedom for all Americans. What you do is honorable. What they do is blessed!

War Story

You may have seen that bumper sticker that reads something to the effect of, "If I'd known how much fun grandkids are, I wouldn't have wasted my time having my children." There's nothing like being a grandparent. Nothing! I've got a grandbaby named Nieves. She's the most incredible, and beautiful little person you've ever seen. No, really! When she and her mom lived with us, one of her favorite things to do first thing in the morning, before her mom took her to the Child Development Center, was to go out with me to put up our flag. I'd take her in one arm and take the flag in the other. We'd go out and place the flag in its holder and she'd caress it for a few minutes. "This is my flag, Opa, "she'd tell me, her little blue eyes twinkling. Eventually, she took to saluting with her right hand as she held the flag with her left. These are the blessings of liberty personified by our future.

That flag inspires pride in me too. And gratitude. I remember being "in the desert" with my troops in a place where we weren't allowed to play the national anthem. Consequently, we couldn't have a retreat ceremony which is one of my favorite military ceremonies. As I mentioned earlier, there are places in the world where you could lose an appendage if you do what you're not "supposed" to do. I don't know about you, but I've grown very attached to each of my body parts.

I was honored to be out in the desert with a couple of First Sergeants who felt the same way I do about retreat ceremonies. I'm not sure who was more frustrated with not being able to do one. They'd been out there longer, so chances are they had me beat. They both complained to me about it and, as usual, I challenged them to do something about it. They did! We did! We decided to risk life and limb, okay, more limb, to have a retreat before we left for home.

The afternoon before we left, one of the Shirts took a metal flag stand and set it in the center of our compound, which, luckily, was four buildings placed in a square configuration. It was possible to see into the compound and that was a risk. The other Shirt had the flag on a staff and the first Shirt had a boom box with a tape of "Retreat" and "The Star Spangled Banner." The Shirt with the flag looked around, kind of like the spy movies you've seen, went out and placed the flag in its stand. The other Shirt and I went out as quickly as we could. All three of us stood retreat, proudly saluting the flag as we played the National Anthem. Luckily, the voltage was 220 so the music was a little faster than usual. We finished retreat and "got the heck out of Dodge," as the saying goes.

In a sense, it was an act of defiance on our part. In a deeper sense it was something we had to do to regain our pride in our country and our service. I've never understood service members running for shelter when they hear the first notes of retreat. That short ceremony, all of maybe three minutes, is a great opportunity to stop whatever it is we're doing and to contemplate the many freedoms we're blessed with. I know we don't have much time to be grateful, but we have to make time for it. If you don't make time, time will ungratefully go its merry way and one day you'll look back wishing you'd started being grateful sooner. Gratitude is everything!

The 212-Degree Challenge

Am I grateful for my blessings today?

- 211-degrees or less

- 212-degrees plus!

Am I grateful for my family?

- 211-degrees or less

- 212-degrees plus!

Am I grateful for my troops?

- 211-degrees or less

- 212-degrees plus!

Am I grateful for my bosses?

- 211-degrees or less

- 212-degrees plus!

Bob Vásquez, CMSgt (Ret), USAF

Lesson 10

Get out of the way!

For most of my enlisted life, I was taught that my job was to work myself out of a job. In other words mentor, train, teach and lead someone to take over for me when I wasn't there or when I was gone for good. I always tried to do that, although I'm not sure I always succeeded. An effective servant-leader will do all that's possible to ensure the success of the unit, consequently, the success of the Force, beyond his or her watch.

Stephen Covey devised a process that I think will help you get to where you can get out of the way and feel comfortable that the mission will be accomplished, if not surpassed. He calls it a Win-Win Agreement. It's a tool that, if you live up to it, will empower your troops to reach their individual potential. There are five parts to it.

First, agree on what your desired result is. For most of my military life, the people who led me never told me what they expected of me. I always had to figure it out, and luckily, my intuition was good enough to accurately guess what my supervisor expected and I did okay. To this day, I can ask troops what their supervisor expects of them and they can't tell me. Their supervisor, however, expects it! Whatever it is. Those troops are held accountable for accomplishing it! Again, whatever it is. Supervisors often assume that their troops know what they should be doing. You know what? They don't! So tell them! And if you really want to be *THE* Chief, inspire them to agree to what it is you want them to aspire to. You and I know all you want from them is their best and they will give it to you. If they agree to do so! It may take some time, but sit next to them, not in front of them, and help them envision their potential. Let them see themselves as the professionals you expect and they will live up to it!

Next, and this is critical, tell them what resources they have available to them. How many times have you started a new job not knowing where anything is? There have been very few times that my predecessor and I were given the opportunity for him or her to train me. It was usually, "Hey, we're glad you're here, now get to work!" I had to figure out for myself where things were, even though I didn't know where I was! What tools will they need? Where are they? Where can they get more, if they need more? How much time do they have to accomplish what you expect? What if they need more time? These are simple things that we assume our direct reports already know. They don't. Again, tell them!

The most important resource a young person can have is you! Great leaders aren't necessarily those with the most ability, but they are those with the most availability. If you make yourself available to help them, they will follow you anywhere! Making yourself available builds trust. But you already know that.

Thirdly, guidelines, or standards, are the meat of our Force. Without them we can accomplish nothing. We're too big and spread out not to have them. But what are they? Okay, you, as a Chief, have been around a little bit. You've heard or figured out all the rules. You have to to work around them. Do you think your troops know as much as you do? If they did, wouldn't they be the chiefs? I've always believed I could work with anyone as long as I knew "where they were coming from." If a commander gave me specific guidelines, it was easy to work within them. What was hard was working for someone who had no rules. Then, I didn't know whether I was on track or not. Guidelines are like a map. The terrain may be sporadic, but if you know where the destination is and you know where the traps are, you can get there a lot easier than if you go at it blindly.

I told you there were five parts. Here's the fourth. We talk about accountability all the time, yet, I'm not sure we know what that means, but I do know we seldom make people accountable. The reason is that we don't have processes for it. Effective accountability requires periodic assessment. We tell our direct reports that they're accountable for accomplishing a task, yet we don't tell them to whom, or when or how, they're accountable. Set that up at the beginning. Most people will live up to deadlines, especially if you both agree to them. The super achievers will surpass those deadlines.

The last tenet is an agreement on consequences. What if your troop does live up to your expectations? What then? Can you provide rewards of some kind? Depending on the maturity of the person, some people really need tangible rewards to feel a sense of accomplishment. Some don't. Some say they don't. Now, if you're thinking that they know that "success is a journey not a destination" get real! It takes a lot of humility and maturity to get to the point where you do what you do for any reason other than the immediate rewards you expect. We're not all the same in what fulfills us. We are the same in that we need fulfillment. Pay attention and figure out what cranks a person's motor and provide it to them. To some it may be time off to be with their family. To others it may be a plaque for their wall. To the very few it will be a pat on the back and a sincere, "Thanks!" Make the time to know your troops and provide them with what makes them happy, not you. The truth is if they're happy accomplishing the mission it will make you happy too. Let them know what they can expect. You already let them know what you expect. Then, live up to it.

One more time, here are the basics of the Win-Win Agreement:

1. Agree to the desired results. What do you want in the end?

2. Tell them where they can get the resources they'll need to accomplish the desired results.

3. Set up an accountability process and stick to it.

4. Establish the guidelines by which you'll both live.

5. Agree to the consequences of success and of failure.

If you develop and employ this Win-Win process you can rest easy in knowing that your troops know what they need to know, that they've agreed to your mutual expectations, and that they will continue the process even when you're not there. I'm reminded of the adage, "Give a man a fish and you feed him for a day. Teach that man to fish and you feed him for a lifetime." Your troops want to be professionals. They want to be accountable. They want to have integrity. Help them out by teaching them what those words mean. Then let them loose! Get out of their way!

This lesson may be the most difficult because no matter how tough you are as a servant-leader, or as a Chief, you're still human. The measure of a leader's effectiveness is in whether everything goes well while he or she is gone. The deep truth is that, although we don't want our troops to fail while we're gone, we do hope that we're missed.

I'm reminded of an Andy Griffith Show episode in which Aunt Bee has to go out of town for a few days and leaves the boys, Andy and Opie, to fend for themselves. As you can imagine, or remember if you've seen the episode, while she's gone, things go a bit awry. Now, Andy, being the great nephew that he is, thinks that what would make Aunt Bee happy is for them to have taken care of themselves without a problem. And he tells Aunt Bee that things are good every time she calls. She's not quite sure she should, but she accepts Andy's assessment. Eventually, Aunt Bee is about to return.

The house is a mess, but Andy and Opie pool their efforts together and clean it up just in time for Aunt Bee's arrival. As she sees that everything is in tip-top shape she begins to feel unneeded. Her self-esteem diminishes. Only after she finds out the truth, that the boys couldn't do without her, that they really did need her, does she regain her composure as she returns to fulfilling her life's purpose, taking care of the house and her boys.

I'm also reminded of the movie, Rudy. The true story of a young boy who envisioned playing on the Notre Dame football team although he was very small. At the end of the movie, after playing a couple of plays, and after sacking the quarterback for a loss, he's carried off the field with the audience chanting, "Ru-dy! Ru-dy!" In the tunnel, his mentor, Fortune, basks in the knowledge that he had something to do with Rudy's success. True servant-leadership at it best!

Get out of the way! Empower your troops to be the best they can be and they will. Share all you have with them and then let them succeed. They will astound you with what they can accomplish. You can take credit for raising them, although you shouldn't take it for what they've done. They know what you've done for them and they'll be grateful. They may not show it at the time, but eventually you'll get that phone call, that e-mail, or that note, thanking you for helping them be their best. All the money in the world can't compare to that payback. And you'll know in your heart that all you did was get out of their way.

War Story

This isn't a war story. It's more a comment on the power of empowerment. I often do an exercise in my seminars where I ask the audience to fill out a card that asks participants to "name two teachers who inspired you to achieve in school, name two friends who helped you through a difficult time, name two people who taught you something worthwhile, name two heroes whose stories have inspired you."

The card is part of what I call an Influencers Quiz. The point is that the people whom participants list are the people who influenced them to be who they are. Invariably, when I ask the audience to share who they listed and why, they always get to how those influencers empowered them by letting them try for themselves.

Remember the final scenes of Rudy where he's being carried off the field? If you've ever been carried off the field you know how great that feels. Earlier I mentioned Fortune, Charles S Dutton's character, and how he felt watching Rudy's success. What feels better than being carried off the field is when one of your protégés is carried off the field.

167

Not long ago, one of my favorite protégés, Jose LugoSantiago, was selected for promotion to Senior Master Sergeant. It just happened that the day the line numbers were released the e-mail system at his base went down. Hey, the lines were clogged with great joy! Anyway, by the end of the day I did receive a note from Jose telling me how he'd been trying to connect with me all day. As I recall, I was teaching that day so he wasn't able to reach me by phone. He'd invested much of his time that day trying to reach me to thank me for his success. His note related to how I'd helped him grow into who he is now. I still have that note in my most prized possessions stash. The truth is that I didn't do anything to help Lugo succeed. All I did was guide him and let him do what he had the potential to do. But his gratitude made my day.

Often, it's easier for us to do what we expect our troops to do. But we can't do it for them. They have to grow so that we can go. I'm totally actualized in that my protégés continue to connect with me and thank me for helping them reach their potential. There's no better feeling than knowing you've helped someone be them. It's often difficult, but you have to let go.

As I mentioned at the beginning of these thoughts, if you aspired to be a Chief because of the celebrity you might enjoy, we picked the wrong person. Sorry, but that's the truth. The real power in being *THE* Chief is that you can nurture and guide youngsters to fulfill their own potential. And they have plenty of it. The key is to give them all you have and then get out of the way. They will surprise you. And, interestingly, they'll tell everyone they know that you are *THE* Chief!

The 212-Degree Challenge

Do my troops know what I expect of them?

- 211-degrees or less
- 212-degrees plus!

Do I know what my troops expect of me?

- 211-degrees or less
- 212-degrees plus!

Are my troops and I in agreement as to where we're going and how to get there?

- 211-degrees or less
- 212-degrees plus!

Have I empowered my troops to reach their potential?

- 211-degrees or less
- 212-degrees plus!

Lesson 11

Think backward!

In Lesson 1, I briefly mentioned the concept of vision. Have you ever known a person of great vision? At the risk of diluting your respect for that person, let me tell you the truth. He or she thought backward. That's nowhere near as bad as it may sound. Thinking backward requires great vision and maybe even some wisdom. Dr Stephen Covey calls it "begin with the end in mind," one of his *Seven Habits of Highly Effective People.*

Every person who ever did anything of consequence thought backward. That is, they envisioned the end result and then devised ways to accomplish their vision. Imagine, if you envision all of your troops as super achievers, as professionals, as people who deserve the trust of the American people, what do you think they'll end up being? Exactly, whatever you think they'll be! Amazing how that works! On the other hand, if you think of them as bums, they'll become bums, because, whether you realize it or not, you'll treat them like bums, because that's how you see them. It's a vicious circle.

At the risk of alienating some of you, let me espouse a thought that I've tried to perpetuate for many, many years. We often refer to our troops as kids. Fellow Warriors, they ain't kids! Yeah, I know they seem like they are at your age. Some of you are really old! Some of you think that they often act like kids. Do you think that they may do so because you call them by that term?

I have kids at home...or I did. I would never have empowered them with multi-million dollar aircraft or other equipment. I would never have let them drive buses or other vehicles that held the risk of killing people. Kids aren't ever appointed publishers of newspapers. Kids don't extract blood from patients. Kids are not worthy of the responsibilities we place on our young Airmen. Have I made my point?

Words are very powerful influencers, Warriors. They are thoughts made manifest in your behavior when you use them continuously. That can work positively if

172

you do it positively, but it works even better when you do it negatively.

For instance, I always refer to Debbie as my lovely-bride-of-twenty-nine-wonderful-and-fulfilling-years. That's a positive thing. Now, I change the year, adding one each year, to make it truthful. That reference becomes an affirmation that becomes truer the more I say it. And I say it a lot!

Again, to call your troops kids means you think of them as such. If you think of them as such your expectations of them will be below the standard of professionals. Is that what you're looking for in your troops? Use your power of vision. See them as professionals, think of them as professionals. Treat them like professionals. I guarantee you, they'll become professionals.

You've probably studied some management theory, particularly McGregor's Theory X and Theory Y. Douglas McGregor theorized that the Xers are bums (my word) and Ys are super achievers (my words). What's bad about that theory is that some folks still buy into the X part of it and make it happen! They'll see people as bad so they'll make them bad. It's the self-fulfilling prophecy in action.

Sometimes what's difficult as a servant-leader is to find the good in everyone you lead. It's most especially difficult, sometimes, to find the good in those you follow. It may take some time and effort, but if you hone your power of vision, and, I believe, the only way to do that is by practicing it, you will empower your troops, and your commanders, to reach their full potential. You may even find that your troops have a lot more to offer than they'll fess up to. You may even find you can offer them a lot more than you thought at first.

Here's a suggestion. Think backward. Make some time every day to envision your troops as the very best in the world. Then think about what it would take for them to be the best, or their best. Then, go help them do it!

War Story

I'm leading my seminar when a young cadet (Okay, they're ALL young!) who has been fidgety all morning finally stops me and says, "Chief, I need to talk to the class!" Being the nice guy that I am, I acquiesce to her request and ask her to stand up and speak.

"Chief," she says, "last semester, when we came to the first part of your seminar you had us fill in our Purpose Card. (Having a purpose is so important that I have my cadets write theirs down so that they can remind themselves why they're at the Academy.) I did as you said, I wrote it down. I didn't do what you asked us to do, though, and that was to put it where we could see it regularly. I put mine away with other books and what not. On my Purpose Card, I'd written down that I wanted to be a Falconer. (Our school mascot is the falcon. Falconers are the team of cadets who travel around the country with our falcons, doing shows and exhibitions.) Chief, since ninth grade I've wanted to be a Falconer. In fact, that's why I came to the Air Force Academy. And that's also why I've stayed here in spite of the trials we've been through.

175

"At the beginning of this semester I received your e-mail telling us to bring our Purpose Card with us to this session. I had to look for mine, but I found it. When I did find it, it reminded me of why I stayed. In order to be a Falconer, however, you have to have a GPA of 2.5 or higher. I didn't make that the first semester. But what I've done this semester is what you said. I put my Purpose Card where I could see it every day. I put it on my desk next to my computer where I do my homework. When I got tired of doing my homework and was ready to quit I'd look over at my Purpose Card and it reminded me why I'm still here. There were days I didn't even want to do my homework, but I'd look at my Purpose Card and it would remind me why I came here to begin with, and I'd do my homework.

"Chief," she went on, "This morning, before I came to VECTOR! (That's the name of my program.) I received an e-mail...I'm on the team! I'm a Falconer!"

She was in tears as the rest of the class stood to give her an ovation. Chiefs don't cry. Our eyeballs sometimes sweat. Mine were sweating just a little as she finished her testimonial.

But wait, there's more! Okay, I know that sounds like an infomercial, but don't change the channel just yet.

My lovely bride of twenty-nine wonderful and fulfilling years (See, I told you I say that all the time!) and I are sitting at our first football game of the new season. (The rest of the semester during which the cadet made her statement passed as did the summer, which I could hardly stand because the cadets go off for nine weeks to parts unknown and I miss them.) We have a tradition that during halftime the Falconers do a short show. They go onto the field and have the falcons fly all over the stadium as they try to hit them with a leather thong. Okay, they tell me they really aren't trying to hit them, but I always ask them, "Does the bird know that?" It seems the falcons avoid the Falconers until they're summoned to join them at center field. I guess you have to be there to really understand.

Anyway, Deb and I aren't paying a lot of attention since we've seen these exhibitions many times and she has to dust off all of the left-over popcorn from the front of my coat during half-time (You get over it after 29 years, guys.). Our eyes are guided back to the field as the PA announcer introduces the Falconer at center field. As he says the name, I'm thinking, "I know that name!" Now, let me tell you that I know every cadet who comes through our Academy because they have to attend my course to graduate. I, unfortunately, don't remember all of their names, there are 4400 of them. I do remember their faces, though. Well, as the announcer introduces the cadet I realize it's the one who had stood up at VECTOR! and shared her story about the power of that Purpose Card!

"Wow," I'm thinking! "She came to the Academy to be a Falconer. She stayed to be a Falconer. She's now, at this moment, in front of thousands of fans, living her purpose! She's literally living her life-long dream! All due to that little piece of card stock. At least, that was the catalyst that ignited the fire in her belly to do what she had to do."

Interestingly, last year we played Army at West Point. (We won, by the way!) Our Falconers went with the team. As we watched the game's halftime show on nation-wide television the cameras were focused on our mascot and the handlers. Guess who was smiling the biggest smile on national TV? Yep, it was her.

The purpose of this story, and, by the way, it's a true story, is to show you how having a purpose will drive you. It may drive you crazy, but it will drive you. Once you find your purpose it will ignite in you an unstoppable passion. That passion has to be guided. It's guided by your vision. That cadet could see herself succeeding before it happened! She saw the end result as a ninth grader. She just had to do what it took to make her dream a reality.

I love my job. It's not a job, really, it's a passion. That's what having a purpose does. If your purpose is to do what you get paid to do, life becomes a joy. To make that purpose real I see myself leading the future Air Force leaders to being their very best. I think backward, seeing my cadets as great officers of character. I know they'll live up to my vision of them. And I try to inspire them to make it their vision of themselves.

I live north of the Academy, in Monument. My home is truly beautiful. As I drive to work every day, on I-25, just before I turn off there's a huge highway sign that reminds me that to get to the United States Air Force Academy I have to turn right a mile ahead. Every time I see that sign my heart beats stronger. That sign serves as my Purpose Card and my vision of success. It reminds me

179

why I do what I do, and let me tell you, I invest a lot of effort and time doing what I do, but it's all worth it. My purpose, literally, drives me to the Academy. My vision guides me to do the right things for the right reasons in the right way. And I love it!

My cadets, by the way, call me *THE* Chief!

The 212-Degree Challenge

Do I see my troops as professionals?

- 211-degrees or less

- 212-degrees plus!

Do I help them see themselves as professionals?

- 211-degrees or less

- 212-degrees plus!

Do I refer to my troops as "Airmen" instead of "kids"?

- 211-degrees or less

- 212-degrees plus!

Do I envision myself helping my troops grow?

- 211-degrees or less

- 212-degrees plus!

Bob Vásquez, CMSgt (Ret), USAF

Lesson 12

Seek help!

You can't be *THE* Chief by yourself. You'll need help. Seek it! One of the best lessons I was taught was from Chief Master Sergeant of the Air Force, Number 11, Dave Campanale. He'd recommended me to be the Senior Enlisted Advisor to the Commander at Fairchild Air Force Base near Spokane, Washington. Shortly after Brigadier General Gary Voellger had hired me, Dave called me to congratulate me and to mentor me. He assured me it would be a tough job. Little did either of us know how tough it was to be. (Ask an old Chief about the hospital shooting and the Buff crash, both in the same week.)

He told me to find someone I could talk to. Someone who had no agenda to succeed me and would be willing to listen and maybe provide some guidance when necessary. I was blessed to find CMSgt Jimmy Theiss who had previously been a Senior Enlisted Advisor at Misawa Air Base in Japan. Our conversations always started with, "Hey, whatcha doin'?" and ended with him admonishing me to persevere. "Hang in there, Bob," Jimmy would always advise, "it'll pass." It always did. Thanks, Jimmy.

I've already told you that a Chief has little authority. But you can develop great power by developing and maintaining relationships with others who have more authority and power. The most effective way to do that is by being humble.

Don't be afraid to ask peers, or followers for that matter, for help. So often, during my active-duty life, I saw Chiefs fall or fail because their pride kept them from seeking help. Many times it was financial help they needed. Oh, I don't necessarily mean asking peers for money, although sometimes that may be the need. Sometimes we get in over our financial heads with investments and bills, and such. Seek help. There are experts out there who are more than willing to help you.

The problems my fellow Chiefs got into, in every case I'm aware of, could have been avoided if others had known. I don't know a Chief who won't give you the proverbial shirt off his or her back if you need it. It may be tough to seek help, but, often, the consequences of not doing so are tougher.

I don't know whether you believe in God or not. The truth is that God exists and you need God's help to get you through your military life, and your personal life, every day. Seek God's help. Often, you do that through prayer. Sometimes it's through talking with chaplains. I know, there aren't enough chaplains to do what we need as a force. At the same time, those chaplains don't know how to say no. (There are some supernatural exceptions to these rules, after all.) Whether it's a chaplain you need or maybe just a friend with a strong sense of spirituality or just some quiet time, seek help!

You'll never find time, so make time for yourself. Reflect on your purpose daily. Assess your behavior and your thoughts often. The Bible quotes Jesus as saying, "The Kingdom of God is within you." All that you've read about in this book is within you. There is nothing new under the sun. My purpose was to inspire you to think about what you already know and to help you use that self-knowledge to improve yourself and those you work and live with.

This entire book is based on the concept of humility. Be humble. Know that none of us is as smart as all of us. Find those who are willing to help, and accept it. Acknowledge their support and help them. Most importantly, pass it on. I call that *HEIRPOWER!*

War Story

(from *Heirpower! Eight Basic Habits of Exceptionally Powerful Lieutenants*, by bob vásquez)

You're going to find this hard to believe, but I can be arrogant when I choose to. Yeah, yeah, I know you're saying, "Say it ain't so, Chief!" I promised you the truth and that's the truth, as much as it hurts you. Let me prove it to you.

I was assigned to the Fifteenth Air Force Band at March Air Force Base in California. It was my first assignment as a Chief Master Sergeant. I was a bit proud of myself. I'd survived some events in my life that others had said would be fatal to my career. I'd beaten the odds and made the highest rank in the Air Force enlisted structure. I was in the top one percent of the enlisted force! I was, to put it in the vernacular, a little "ate up" with myself.

In almost twenty years of service as a musician, I'd never had the opportunity to go home to play for my folks. "My folks" was all those countless hundreds of people who lived in Deming, New Mexico and whose last names ended in "uez." That opportunity came shortly after I arrived at March. The band hadn't toured near my hometown so my commander suggested I take the big band there to show some "home-boy-makes-good" pride. Great idea!

Since that area of the Southwest was my turf, I decided to do the advance work, just to ensure a successful tour. I went out to several small towns in southern New Mexico. Okay, all towns in southern New Mexico are small! Anyway, Deming was my last stop before returning to March. I did my work and stayed an extra day to be with my family. I hadn't seen some of my boys in years so I went out searching for them. I was amazed at how many of my high school friends were still in town. High school, by the way, was a great experience for me. Best six years of my life! Hey, I was an overachiever!

As I told you at the beginning of this story, I can be arrogant. Look, my buds made me be that way. They'd gone nowhere in the past 20 years. Richey and Eddie Sainz, Hector Ochoa, Richard Acosta, Charlie Sera had all stayed in our little dinky home town doing what their dads had done all of their lives, which is what their dads' dads had done before. I, on the other hand, had already seen the world. I'd played for all of the Presidents of the United States alive at the time! I'd been overseas! Man, I'd been to Burma! I was worldly! How could I not be arrogant? See? My friends made me that way! I enjoyed visiting with my old chums, but we just weren't the same any more. I was in a different league now. I went back to California to coordinate the tour that would show my folks how good I'd done.

We started the tour in northern Arizona and worked our way to central New Mexico. It was winter and the weather didn't seem to want to cooperate with us. Not only did we have to load in and out in the cold and wet, but it was long stretches of nothing but desert between towns we played. We played at Eastern New Mexico University near Silver City one night and left for New Mexico State University in Las Cruces the next morning. We were scheduled to perform there that evening. What a blustery day! We were traveling in an MCI bus, carrying about 25 people, and an 18-wheel trailer carrying tons of musical and electronic equipment. The equipment truck drove in front of us.

As we traveled down this two-lane winding highway through the middle of nowhere we noticed the equipment truck, a few miles ahead of us, had pulled over to the side. There wasn't much of a shoulder but the driver had gotten out of the way as best he could. Wouldn't you know it? All four cars registered in New Mexico happened to drive by that truck that day! It was a tough situation. It was raining and cold. The truck, and now the bus, was hindering traffic. You see, those four guys had never seen a situation like this so they had to keep coming around to see what was happening.

The truck was hard broke. That's a term airplane mechanics use that means "that vehicle ain't goin' nowhere!" This was the days before anyone had ever asked, "Can you hear me now?" We had no cell phones, and no way, other than to drive a hundred miles, to get to a phone to call for help. Luckily, a local sheriff stopped to help and carried me and an assistant to his office to call for a wrecker to come out to save us.

It seems there were now more than four cars registered in New Mexico and they were all busted too. Every local wrecker I called was out and wouldn't be back for hours. I didn't have time to wait. The sheriff suggested calling a wrecker from the nearest town,

Deming. If you were paying attention, you'll remember that Deming is my hometown.

I had no choice. I called Deming. The only wrecker in town. Sainz' Wrecker Service. Richard Sainz, proprieter. Richey answered my call. Again, if you were paying attention you'll recognize the name of one of my old buds.

"Hey, Bobby!" he said after I announced myself, "How are you?" Well, we talked about more than just what I was in need of, but we did get to that point. I needed his help and I needed it quickly. As we finished our conversation, Richey said, "I'll be right there!" And he was! I don't know how he got there so quickly, but he got there fast. Maybe it had something to do with all of the state cops being family, consequently not having to worry about speeding.

On our way back to the truck and bus I got to thinking.

Here I was, a top dog in my society, the Air Force. I commanded literally thousands of troops, had almost countless resources at hand, had done things I can't tell you about without having to shoot you, all in all a highly successful life, yet I was stuck with my team in the middle of the desert and the only person who was available to help me was a skinny unpretentious guy whom I had recently looked down on for not doing "more" with his life.

You'll recall all my allusions to humility. I was humbled to the bone. My friend, Richey, a humble man himself, had come to my rescue and, in a sense, rescued the entire United States Air Force by getting us to where we had to accomplish our mission. That truck had major problems but with the help of a few humble men, we accomplished the mission and were able to return to our home base safely. I'm grateful for the help I was provided.

The 212-Degree Challenge

Am I humble enough to ask for help when I need it?

- 211-degrees or less

- 212-degrees plus!

Do I know who to go to for help?

- 211-degrees or less

- 212-degrees plus!

Do I make time for myself regularly?

- 211-degrees or less

- 212-degrees plus!

Do my troops know they can come to me for help?

- 211-degrees or less

- 212-degrees plus!

Bob Vásquez, CMSgt (Ret), USAF

Closing Thoughts

There's nothing like being a Chief! As I said at the beginning, everybody wants to be a Chief, but only a few are chosen. You're one of them. I recall one of the last scenes in the movie titled Saving Private Ryan where Tom Hanks is dying and he's talking to Private Ryan. He tells the young man for whom many sacrificed their lives in order to bring him home safely, "Earn this!" Such is my charge to you. Earn this. You're now a Chief. Do what it takes to really be worthy of those stripes you wear on your sleeve. Wear those stripes in your heart. But remember you have to earn them every day.

My great friend and mentor, DJ Eagle Bear Vanas, author of The Tiny Warrior, often talks about the power of being a chief. As you know from the Foreword he wrote for me for this book, DJ is Odawa Indian and he knows his stuff. He says that in Native American culture, the chief has to be unanimously selected. In other words, everyone has to agree to follow him or her. Imagine if your troops had the opportunity to vote for their chief. Would they select you? I'm convinced that if you do what you just read about you'll have a better chance of being selected unanimously than if you just go on your own. Someone once said, "Learn from others' mistakes, you don't have enough time to make them all yourself." Take what I've given you, mistakes and all, and grow into your own potential.

As I close, let me share with you the only poem I know. Don't worry, it's short, like my attention span, but I think it puts this whole book in perspective. It was written by American author and clergyman Edward Everett Hale. It's titled Duty.

I am only one, but I am one.

I cannot do everything, but I can do something.

And because I cannot do everything

I will not refuse to do the something that I can do.

What I can do, I should do.

And what I ought to do, by the Grace of God,

I will do!

I hope that you will become *THE* Chief! I also hope that you will take what you learn and pass it on to others. The web Chief Seattle referred to will become stronger by the right things we do today and by helping others prepare to do the right things tomorrow. Take courage! Make this a GREAT day!

May the Lord bless you and keep you.

May the Lord make His face shine upon you and be gracious to you.

May the Lord turn His face toward you and give you peace.

¡HEIRPOWER!

bob vásquez!

Made in the USA
Coppell, TX
09 December 2020